HOTEL TANGO 23

'RESPONDING TO THE UNKNOWN'

BENJAMIN PEARSON

WITH

PATRICIA SUTCLIFFE

You Tube Channel - Ben Pearson 'Interceptor'
Twitter - @bs_pearson
www.patriciasutcliffeauthor.com

ISBN–9798541346459

Disclaimer

Some names and details in this book have been
changed to protect anonymity

DEDICATION

I dedicate this book to my Mum & Dad

Stephen and Irene Pearson

'Thank you for building in me the strength of

character to survive'

Thank you also to my family and friends who

have, and

still continue to be there for me

ACKNOWLEDGEMENTS

Patricia Sutcliffe–

www.patriciasutcliffeauthor.com

(My co-author, for making this possible)

Steve Horsfall

Prodoto Commercial Photographic Studios

(For his amazing photograph)

Dan Stanek

(For producing an excellent book cover)

Publicist

(You know who you are)

Chris Ormondroyd

(For his friendship and editing)

Foreword

'Handcuffed Emotions–A Police Interceptor's Drive into Darkness' was the first book in this thought-provoking trilogy. Showing that bravery goes far beyond the duty of a police officer and into their very souls. For Ben, telling his story was a major turning point and braver than any actions he had taken as a bobby. Baring your soul for all to see goes far beyond the duty of a job and into the very personal, well hidden, depths of your very being.

Ben's first book emphasised the crippling effects of PTSD, talking openly about the consequences on family, friends, and job. The feedback from the book has more than shown the good that writing it did, not only for Ben, but for others suffering from mental illness, unseen and debilitating as it is.

So why a second book? Simple people have asked for it. What is different is the realisation that talking about PSTD and any mental illness, in whatever form it takes, is important, but just as important is that sufferers feel they can talk about it without repercussions? To do this, we need to continue to talk out and remove the social stigma. This book seeks to do that. Hotel Tango 23, a call sign Ben will never forget, looks at why we don't talk. Through his stories, some humorous, some reflective, all relevant, we see how the force has changed from the times when the human side of a police officer was at the forefront, the days of the old beat bobby, to times where practices, procedures and tactics have mechanised policing and along with it, some of its humanity.

Society has changed, attitudes have changed, the nature of criminal activity has changed, but the need to talk has not and never will. The stories of Ben and others like him, need to be told and organisations across the board need to recognise that whilst physical injuries are easy to sympathise with, mental illnesses are often under the radar. Only through talking are we able to bring it into the light.

'I think a hero is an ordinary individual who finds strength to persevere and endure in spite of overwhelming obstacles.

Christopher   Reeve

Chapter 1–Releasing the Valve

I sat crying in the front room of my house. I was looking out of the window. The street was empty. There was a bleakness about it I hadn't noticed before. It overcame me with a loneliness that was eating away at me from inside. Normally, I would have been out on duty, hell bent on catching criminals as I had done for the past 19 years. Now, it was all over for me. Everything had come crashing down, and I didn't want to face it.

I could prevaricate no longer; I was mentally ill, and I had to come to terms with all of what that meant. My memory wasn't the same, and I feared I was losing all that had been important to me over all those years. I was in danger of forgetting my memories, both good and bad, along with my identity as a police officer. It was hitting me harder than I thought. I was no longer part of the force, part of the team. I was one of the many unemployed, a statistic! My self-respect was at rock bottom. 'Why me?' A question I asked myself repeatedly, prompted no actual answer. The fog clouding my mind obscured any attempt to make sense of my life and blocked any possible answers to my queries.

My mind was telling me to go back to bed, to forget it all, but I knew that my heart was telling me differently. I had faced a massive setback, but I still had choices. I could sit on my butt and sink into a dark lonely emptiness or do something about it. I had been told I couldn't work until I was well, and that could take years. I had no proper direction, but I had two young children and a loyal partner. I had to speak out. I needed to speak out.

I thought through the conversations with Paul, my therapist, over the past year. His advice was: 'If you can't speak about it, write about it.' At that stage in my illness, I couldn't speak about it, I was still coming to terms with it, understanding it. A brain injury from several years ago was playing its part alongside the PTSD, and I was getting increasingly frustrated.

I smiled a knowing smile and remembered how the team used to look after me. Had I been at work, there would have no question. It was an unwritten rule that whoever I was working with would help write the statements. The thought that I, dyslexic as I was, would do that was just a no no. I would be the first to get physical, hands on and dirty, but the last to take a statement or fill out forms requesting blood samples. Under pressure, my eyes don't see the right words, my brain confuses letters. I can't distinguish between B, D, P, G or J. Numbers were getting mingled in with simple words or letters. E's became 3's and they would float about on the page. Then, becoming embarrassed and pressurised, I would stutter or slur. Teamwork spared me from that, and I was eternally grateful. Now I had no team, they were someone else's team now. I was on my own, alone, so how would I get the words out?

In the force we often took teamwork for granted. Like the time I arrested a drunk driver and was on my own. I knew there would be forms to fill in and that I would struggle, but

John, in another car, was aware of our unwritten rule. He radioed me laughing. Knowing I would struggle he offered his services. It was a running joke, but one shared with me, not against me. I was secure and had a huge support bubble. Now I was being told to write again, only this time it wasn't a simple form, a statement or blood documents, it was so much more important. I was writing to cleanse myself of all the bad and painful experiences that haunted me.

'Use a computer' was the sound advice from my psychiatrist. It was the only way I could help myself, and somehow, I had to become a teammate with my laptop. I would concentrate on the words; it would deal with the spellings and corrections. With the help of my new best friend, I began. I sat there; a word document opened before me. It was as blank as my mind, nothing there, it had all disappeared. I wanted desperately to remember and tried to get something down on paper. The only things coming into my head were words like FUCK, BOLLOCKS, SHIT. I became incredibly frustrated and almost gave up.

If you have never done it, it is so hard to sit at a computer and author a book. My mind went away from me; all I could see were those little black boxes filled with pain, sitting on the shelf in my deepest soul. I tried to remember the things that happened to me. With each event I typed, a floating red line beneath a word would appear to tell me I'd made a mistake; I'd spelled something wrong, or my grammar was poor. I became less confident; I was about to log off and come back another day when something triggered. My fingers were moving faster than they had ever moved. The flood gates opened. The levels of anger, frustration, love and joy were overwhelming. Story after story exploded onto the page: foot chases, fights, multiple stabbings and murders. I felt like I was writing a cross between 'Harry Potter,' 'Smokey and the Bandit' and 'The Bill'. I lost full control. Facts merged with fiction; false memories with actual memories, I couldn't tell what was real and what wasn't.

I was baring my soul, but I knew it was a positive way to channel my energy. I had a strange feeling of being alive again. Seeing my thoughts and feelings laid out on paper blew me away. The very thing I feared before was now becoming my friend, opening my mind and cleansing me in a way that I never imagined could happen. I was seeing a direction that I had to go in, and I wanted to get there at full speed, just like on a blue light run.

Now it's one thing getting your memories onto paper, but it's another to turn them into a book. To me, writing a book would be like teaching an elephant Japanese, it was never going to happen. Then for some strange reason, you come across Dumbo wearing a kimono and he greets you with 'Konichiwa.' You realise anything is possible if you want it badly enough.

I approached Chris, the father of one of my best friends. He was a very talented man who had authored his own books. Local publications 'Windhill Tales' and 'Hippies, Vandals and an Alien Called Pete' had been local hits for him. I had a long conversation with him about what it would mean to write about my experiences. He gave me encouragement and told me that a book about PTSD could help so many people and would be good for my mental health as well. 'Leave it with me; I'll see what I can do, he said.'

I needed help, and he knew it. It's just the same as if someone asks me 'do you know Phil from West Midlands

Police?' I would give them a blank look. But ask me if I know a good officer who dealt with rape cases and I'd reply, yes, I can give you a name and number to get you the help you need. That's what Chris did. A few days later he contacted me and told me about a lady called Pat Sutcliffe who wanted to help me. Pat was a writer who had authored her own books, but she was also a CBT counsellor. She would understand the emotions I would experience, pull out the best and worst of me, and help me on the journey to get a book finished. We made contact and became great friends.

Hours upon hours Pat and I spent together, days turned to weeks, weeks to months. There was crying, talking, recording and writing. Slowly and frequently, painfully, it poured out, and a book was forming. It was amazing. My dad's words came back to me so many times. 'You do not know what you know until someone asks you.' Pat pulled and tugged the stories out of me. One led to another, the drama, love and pain, all embroiled in one. I ate, slept, and thought about the experiences. The trauma of losing my parents, the hate I felt about my illness, but then the peace I felt getting it all out.

Within several months, the book that was to be only a memoir came to life and 'HANDCUFFED EMOTIONS' was born. Pat told me that such a book would make a real difference to others who were going through the hell I was experiencing. I didn't believe her, but she was right. The reaction to the book has been phenomenal, as you will see later, but for now it's enough to say that whilst I think it clearly outlined the horror of PTSD. I feel it falls short of the importance of speaking out. There is so much more I want to share about stories from the past, and my future journey with a mental illness. All this is rolled up into 'HOTEL TANGO 23'.

The first question that springs to mind is why we don't talk openly about mental health? Why is it such a voodoo subject? We talk about physical injuries with no problems. The obvious answer to this has its roots in history. The development of lunatic asylums played a massive part in public perception about people who were mentally ill. A place named 'Bedlam', built as early as 1247, now a general hospital, raised income by allowing the public to pay to watch the lunatics.

Radical and often gruesome, so-called medical experts had developed physical therapies by the start of the 20th century. Therapies such as insulin shock, Cardiazol shock and frontal lobotomy were used to treat the mentally insane. Stanley Royds in Wakefield didn't close until 1995, and High Royds, the former West Riding Pauper Lunatic Asylum, in 2003. I actually can't believe I'm writing about High Royds. When I was a young man, tiling in my father's company, we worked at High Royds. I remember a nurse following me around, opening and locking doors to give me access to the building. I remember tiling part of a floor in the corridor. Both doors locked at either end, but patients stood there, just looking at me through the glass in the door, blank looks on their faces. I was so freaked out it was untrue. It felt like I had stepped back in time 200 years.

In places like this, padded cells were also common. Names such as imbecile, nutcase, lunatic, mental case and nut job were used to describe anyone who was suffering from a mental illness. Phrases, the likes of, 'Talk like that and you'll end up in the nuthouse' or 'You're bonkers, get yourself seen to...' and 'ignore him, he's a crackpot.' We have all heard similar statements before. Is there no surprise then that people who have a mental illness are afraid to talk about it?

Would I have talked about my struggles earlier? Spoken out before it got to the stage where its impact left me so destroyed and downtrodden that I lost the career I loved and my self-esteem? It's unlikely. The stigma associated with mental illness was too great.

I'd be lying if I said that no one ever opened up about mental illness to me. Looking back, I feel ashamed to say that I would have probably been one of those who, whilst offering to help on the surface, inside I would think 'get a grip'. Back then, I had a closed view of what mental illness really meant. I saw what I saw without seeing or knowing the full picture.

I can recall clearly two who opened up to me. Out of love and respect for them, their names will remain private. I don't want any labels placed on them. They will know who they are, and that's enough to let them know I'm sorry, I didn't take them more seriously.

The first was a man I sometimes worked with. He was sitting at a table with me one day and told me he was struggling. He had just lost a family member. I was typing a statement and doing my utmost to focus on what I was writing against the backdrop of a busy and noisy office. Sweaty arsed cops were everywhere, shouting, laughing at jokes, they were just releasing tension which was normal.

It was then that the bloke got really close to me and poured out his feelings. I talked to him, reassured him, and gave him support, but inside I was thinking, 'I'm a traffic cop, I'm not trained to deal with this. I've my own problems in life.' I looked up and saw tears in his eyes. I stopped typing and tried to focus on the discussion, but I felt very uncomfortable. As I look back, I tell myself that I handled it okay, but in honesty, I could have given a lot more.

I was just the same as anyone else, I'd be there, I'd listen but not really understand. I may even give a friendly cuddle, but I didn't. I know now, facing mental illness, that a cuddle could have meant so much to him, were the setting a more private one, I think I would have given him a hug, but it wasn't. I was in an office full of hard-nosed cops. If I could go back in time, or if it was now, I wouldn't give a fuck what people thought of me. I would stand up, wrap my arms around him and tell him I would be there no matter what. I'm just so sad that it had to take my illness to make me see that.

On the second occasion it was a lad I worked with, a genuine star. He had lost both his parents young and suffered a bad upbringing but remained focused and strong. He is an excellent officer and outright, good lad and great father. One night we were out in the car together, he opened up and told me what was going on in his life. Shocked, but growing in my understanding of people, I knew it had taken a lot for this lad to trust me enough to speak about his problems. He needed comfort and to know I was a friend who would listen without judgment. I won't say more about our conversation that evening other than to thank him wholeheartedly for having my back and sticking by me throughout this journey. You know who you are, so thank you, my friend. I love you.

It's a thing in our society that when someone stops you and asks, 'how are you?' we reply, 'I'm fine, how are you?' It's a

British thing. We don't want to know about all your problems, we have our own. It's like having an unwritten rule that we abide by. The same is true in the force. You pass your time telling your colleagues you are okay, you tell jokes, comment on events, laugh about incidents but you don't say, 'I need help.' Most officers wouldn't know what to do if you did. You hear this time after time in the police, "if I don't laugh, I'll cry". You try to keep your spirits up, but if you can't, you end up in tears. Ask yourself…. 'Why is that?'

For me, I can't ever remember not being a uniformed officer when someone has told me something private and personal. I recall many 'so called' private confessions told to me by criminals trying to get away with their crimes. 'Officer, I don't know why I did it. My mother recently died' or 'My little brother is ill, I needed to get some money'. Sure, I believe you totally. I guess you become hardened to what you are told as a bobby and even then, none of the excuses I have heard over the years come close to someone using mental illness as one. Even criminals shy away from talking about that subject.

It's only when they feel proud of their achievements that people want to tell you about it, even if you are about to arrest them. I remember one time; I stopped a famous footballer in the Wrose area of Shipley. He was a young lad, around 20, and wasn't wearing his seat belt. I went up to his Vauxhall Astra and spoke to him. It was becoming clear to me that every time I asked his name and occupation for the ticket; he grinned from ear to ear. Proudly, he told me his name and said that he was a professional sports person. Okay, I hadn't a Scooby Doo who he was and didn't care. He was breaking the law.

'Can you please sign the ticket?' I asked.

'Why officer, if you wanted my autograph, all you had to do was ask me.'

He expected me to know who he was and was more than happy to play a guessing game with me, even with the clues he gave, I still did not know. Confused, I asked him why he would think I wanted his autograph. There was an awkward silence. I continued following procedure, conducted a person and driving license check, and released the man from the scene. Seconds later, my radio went ballistic. People were trying to contact me from all over the force. Had I got his autograph? Had I got a photo? They asked. The answer to both was no. It turned out he was a major player in one of the biggest teams and world famous. Now he was more than happy to talk, but only about things that were positive

So why do I write? It's because to me it has become my way of talking. I do it to clear my soul. It gives me renewed strength to face my mental illness. Perhaps anyone can sit behind a keyboard and pretend they are superhuman, slagging off people they don't understand. 'Keyboard warriors,' I call them. The people who take joy out of ridiculing others. Those who revert to calling people nutters, idiots, and crackpots when they don't agree with their point of view. That's not writing, nor is it helpful to anyone with mental illness.

To me, I lose myself in my words. They don't talk back to me or try to excuse themselves, and they don't put me down. There are no distractions or negativity. Even when I am writing about things that are negative, I'm now in control. If I don't like what I have written, I can erase it. If it gets too bad,

I can close it down, shut the lid, and return at a better time where my mind's my friend again. If you are reading this book, I want to explain further. Once I write, I find it hard to stop my thoughts; the stories pour out, and I feel like I'm controlling my illness. It's my main way of dealing with what I've lost that I had no choice about it.

Imagine that someone comes into your house and removes your treasured possessions, memories, loved ones, friends, colleagues. How would you react? I'll now add in and change the way people see or view you. Now think about the way they look at you and the difference in their conversation with you. I'll now ask you to write about it. What do you think happens? How does it make you feel?

Then there is the downside, and here my self-doubt comes in. My mind stops being my friend and I think no one is really interested in what I have to say. I'm trying to talk out, but I'm struggling. No one is here to advise me. I know I have a lot to say, but is it interesting enough, what if I overstep the mark? What if I offend people or just write absolute shit? I know I have lots to say, but am I really helping others? Is it helping people to speak about mental illness? And who do I think I am to do that? I'm not qualified!

I lived 19 years in a totally regimented way. I was told how to cut my hair, bull my boots, and not to have personal views. Don't write that on Facebook; don't speak to that person. You can't have tattoos. All this stops your growth as a person. Your views become restricted, and you find it harder to express your thoughts and opinions. To give an example, the police will not give you permission to have a friendship with a known criminal. That's fine, I understand why, but what if someone did something in the silliness of his youth; paid his dues, served his time, and has worked hard for the past ten years tackling knife crime and dealing with youth rehabilitation. To an officer, he is still classed as a criminal, and I couldn't associate with him. Isn't it time we changed our views? Good people can make mistakes.

Well, I sometimes feel like that about my mental illness. I wonder if people see me differently, and at what point do they assess that I'm not mentally ill anymore? Will they change their view about me then? Therefore, I need to write, and I keep telling myself if I change opinions about mental illness in just one person, I've done a worthwhile thing. There is a genuine need to open hearts and minds to many things, not just mental illness.

What you see is not always what you get. I'll try my best to elaborate on this statement, but from an officer's point of view. Last week I went to buy something at a local shop. As I got there, I noticed a group of youths in the car park. Now they don't know I'm retired, and why should they? So, I get out of my car and walk across the car park to the taunt, 'Officer what are you doing?' followed by 'Braap, Braap.' They are making the sound of a gun to give an impression they are bad asses. 'Officer, where's the 330?' So it continues. It's easy to tell that these kids are no strangers to the inside of a prison cell. I go into the shop and when I come out, I go over to them. You could see the shock on their faces as I approached. 'Where's your Glock, then? Come on, show me 9 caps, Braap Braap' They are nice kids, well, okay kids. They just want to have some banter with me, find out how I'm doing. Don't misunderstand. Once I walked away, they would have been talking about who could smash me or knock me out first.

The point I am making is that being a police officer, following the many rules, has kept me from making progress in my life and hindered my treatment of both myself and others. It brings out one of my fears about speaking up. Those who are still under the force umbrella and codes of conduct somehow suffer, so that's what I write about. They still dare not speak out; they have seen what has happened to me by reading my first book.

I know that there are wheels in motion now to re-assess the police's mental health policy. I think they have taken something from my case and really hope they listen and make the needed changes. I would love certain procedures to be put in place; trust and understanding, for two. If you fuck up, they need to learn how to treat someone who is struggling and crying out for help. I must be their poster boy for how they got it so wrong.

I felt that there was no trust, no confidentiality. Everyone was too busy covering their own back. Making 'Joe Public' happy came before looking after the officers and staff. Let's make sure the sergeant or inspector are okay and then fuck everyone else. No one really understood my issues, I may as well have said, 'hello doctor, an African Jumbo Baluma snake has bitten me on my left ass cheek. It's so rare there are only 12 of them in the world'. 'Sorry, I'm not trained for this', said the doctor, 'but hang on, let me put it out over the tannoy speakers. DING, DONG, all personnel beware, we have an ass snake bite in room 2. Come over and have a look.'

What should happen? There needs to be a system whereby I could have gone to a safe room; away from face-to-face contact and speak to someone who fully understands where I am at. An emergency referral should follow that for seeing a specialist, so you could start treatment ASAP. But last, and perhaps just as important, someone to say, 'don't worry about your job, your skills, your place on the team, your ability to pay your mortgage, it's all safe and will be taken care of no matter how long it takes to get you back on your feet.'

In my last days and weeks, I faced something totally different. The lack of caring from the job just astounded me. My permits were withdrawn and being in such a dark place in my mind, I spoke with a Sgt. who was acting up in the post at Headquarters. He said, don't worry, you won't need your permits in FCMU (Call handling)'. The Force's answer to everything was if you couldn't do your job for any reason, they would just move you to the shittiest job imaginable just to get you out of the way. I was about to be kicked off traffic for doing nothing wrong, apart from being ill, and made to sit in a dark room answering 999 calls. This was with no consultation or concern about how that would affect me. Not looking at the problems or issues which have caused my illness, and no thoughts for my mental health. They may as well just put a big sign on my head saying, 'mentally incapable.'

Chapter 2 - Where's my Heartbeat?

Over the past 19 years of service, I have been asked so many times, 'how has policing changed in your time in the force?' And 'would you join now?' Wow, what questions. Let's go back to the start of my dream to join the force. An old TV series called 'Heartbeat' was broadcast on Sunday nights. I remember watching it with my mum and dad when I was a child. The local beat bobby was always there, fighting crime in the Yorkshire Dales; looked up to and respected by all but the most ardent criminal. He was a pillar of the local community, and a friend of the people.

Sadly, I'm talking about the 60s and times change, along with social norms and accepted behaviour. The times when a bobby could stand and chat, get to know the characters in the neighbourhood, is long gone. The once highly visible and accessible beat cop has now become inaccessible, an invisible presence behind the wheel of a fast car.

Not only has society changed, but in line with it, the use of guns and knives, drugs and an array of deadly weapons. Stab vests are now compulsory wear for all officers, along with a host of personal protective equipment strapped around your waist. The police uniform now resembles a military kit rather than the old shirt, slacks, and tie that are most remembered from days long ago. It's as much for the safety of the officer wearing it, as it is for the arrest of criminals.

Communities have also changed from yesteryear. People don't know each other anymore. Doors and windows always remain locked in fear of being a victim. They taught youngsters in the past to respect their elders. Often, granny and granddad lived next door or nearby; aunts and uncles were across the road. Socialising with each other was the norm. Now it's the opposite. Families live and work away from each other and face isolation. Lots of elderly people are left to fend for themselves, and respect has gone out of the window.

You even hear officers saying the jobs fucked. If I was young now, would I join? 'No, I wouldn't,' is my answer. Not because the job is a shit job, it isn't. It's a great job, but there are so many changes taking place every day. There are only so many times you can re-invent the wheel and have top supervisors who just don't care. Some change is necessary and beneficial, but a lot isn't. I also feel that I have missed so many opportunities in my life by becoming married to the job. My biggest regret is not seeing the world more in my younger days to experience more culture; but that's the only mistake I made.

We spend our school years being a kid, doing kids' things with no pressure or worry. Then, suddenly, you are out in the big wide world. You are told 'grow up,' 'act your age,' 'take responsibility,' 'be accountable,' 'You're not little Benny anymore.' Expectations change and things become serious. Forty years down the line, you've worked, paid your taxes and feel shafted by the system. By 'retirement,' you're a broken shell of your former self or totally fucked off with life.

Few are really prepared for retirement. At 44 years of age, I'm not prepared and don't want to be.

I don't want to become the grumpy old man in the street, telling kids not to play by his garden or warning them to 'keep off my grass.' We have enough of those moody sods already, and you all know who you are. When you are young the last thing you want to be is the 'party pooper,' but I realise now that when my doubts descended, I was halfway there. I'm finding my old self now that I'm away from the job. I'd like to think that when I grow old, I will be the one who is seen riding his grandson's skateboard, with the neighbours laughing at me, saying, 'Christ, he's going to break his hip. Silly old sod, act your age.'

So, what would I tell anyone asking me what the best job in the force is? I've thought about this so much in recent months as I've re-lived my time in the role. Well, do you want to know a secret? The best job in the force is not firearms, traffic, or the helicopter unit. Most serving officers with over 15 years' service will tell you the best job is when they were on foot patrol.

I can remember the time when I got to the nick for my shift, did what I needed to do in the station, and got my kit out, put my helmet on with pride, and set off walking. An officer on the beat, a foot bobby, I stood out in the crowd, not simply because I'm 6'2" tall, but because members of the public could see my helmet passing through the crowds. It gave them reassurance. I was important in the local community. Each foot officer had standing and had an aura of safety around them that people warmed to. I knew shop keepers and local shoppers by name. The fishmonger, the butcher, that young lad at the café, who always gave me a cuppa. Alice at the new agents; they were all brilliant people. I remember the 'aged 60 plus group,' who would say. 'Doesn't he look young?' You can't recreate that; the feeling was glorious.

They sent me with a bobby called Dave, the first day I went on foot patrol. He was older than me and had been a beat cop for a year. To me, he had a mature head on his shoulders. It's no surprise he's now an Inspector at Bradford. I'll never forget the first thing he did. He took me past a large shop window where I could see our reflections. He said 'now you have to learn to slow down and walk properly. It takes skill to do the officer walk.' I laughed then as I thought he was taking the piss; I still think it's funny to this day. Now you know where it comes from when people say, 'he walks like a bobby.' It doesn't matter whether you are in Majorca on holiday or sat in some café, the comments will be the same. They can tell, and it's true; hands by your side or behind you, back straight, chin slightly raised, followed by the sweeping of the left leg, then the right leg, one mph slower than everyone else. Why? Well how else can you watch people and observe what's going on?

A priceless facet of being a beat bobby was the ability to interact with the public, being able to talk to both young and old. You could sort out issues on the spot, but most people just wanted to ask how you were, and what the job was like. They really cared about you. They felt they knew you personally. They introduced their children and grandchildren to you as the good man, who they should approach if they ever got lost or needed help.

Today, officers are often single crewed. They are moving from job to job as quickly as they can. Their interaction with the public is extremely limited, unless it's with Chantel and

Barry who are 'kicking off.' Barry has forgotten the chicken dippers but remembered his six cans of Special Brew; Chantel isn't amused. You spend your day alone, inside your car, with the police radio constantly beeping. There's no camaraderie here, you are on your own, no one to talk to, to discuss what's happening in your own life. You are just sitting there, waiting to respond to a job, but you never know what it will be. It must affect your thought processes and the way you look at life.

Rules, regulations, lack of funding, and changing crime patterns have all changed the way police officers work. They have massively reduced the officer's decision-making abilities. When I started, you would go to a job, deal with it and bounce on to the next. For example: Friday night, two men scrapping outside a nightclub. You would separate the two, throw one to the left, one to the right, and tell them to fuck off home. They would go, tails between their legs. Five minutes was all it took, job sorted, and you moved onto the next one.

Those days disappeared a long time ago. Now you follow a very different procedure. It goes like this: I arrest both parties; I seize CCTV, if available. We take statements from those who will give them. Most are so pissed they can't remember their own name, never mind what happened. Then the incident must go onto the police system, before you make your report. Hours later, you're ready for an early interview. Interviews conducted; then 'custody' would release the pair of 'piss heads' at 11am next day. Nine hours, tying up two police officers, and the result? An adult caution; what a pointless exercise and waste of resources.

It's pathetic; they take away your judgement and responsibility. Your ability as a trained officer, and fully grown adult, who can make a reasonable decision, gone. Instead, I am required to phone the HUB. A sergeant and an inspector will sit there, with less experience or service than I have, to decide on my behalf. In most cases, that will be to ARREST. Why? They are so fearful nowadays of something going wrong, too frightened to say you can handle this yourself. It's like working at McDonald's, but having to ask the manager every time someone orders a burger on the drive through, 'boss, can I serve this man?'

The wheel, as I said earlier, has been re-invented so many times, each change more costly than before. A new 'top brass' will come in and issue an order that all patrol cars are to be based at the station where the control room is. This is how things are dealt with, until another boss comes in a few months later, and it all changes back to how it was. Hundreds of thousands of pounds to take it back to the way it was previously. After 19 years in the job, you've experienced 'every which way' the same thing can be done. You know what works and what doesn't but can do nothing about it. The frustration is debilitating.

I must add that this happens so often that officers, including myself, become so pissed off and angry. Leave it alone, we all think, for fuck's sake. Things like closing a station and making us travel a further six miles with a prisoner to another station, only to re-open the same station they closed earlier. It really makes your blood boil. I used to say if Sir Alan Sugar walked in, he would shake his head in disbelief, order it closed, and say it's unfit for purpose, and a drain on public money.

Not all changes were for the worse though, there were some beneficial ones. Improvements in technology gave us the ability to have PNC (Police National Computer) on our hand-held devices, so we could carry person and vehicle checks at crime scenes. Fingerprint machines in our cars meant that no matter how hard a suspect lied to us, we knew the truth, making them look stupid. It's just a joke when, even though we can clearly identify a person in seconds, they keep the denials going, and we end up taking an hour and a half to sort it out. That's the sheer stupidity of some humans.

I recall my tutor, John and I, on patrol one night in Shipley. It was around 9pm when we stopped a car that showed up as having no insurance on PNC, and on our in-car ANPR (Automatic Number Plate Recognition) system. John and I had been exchanging the usual stories that bored coppers tell each other when the car's number plate flashed up. We asked the driver to get into our car for questioning. He was a young Asian male, no older than 20. Totally baby-faced, the type of lad who doesn't even shave or have spots yet.

Now every officer has had the 'EH–WHAT MAN?' in their car. These lads are ten-a-penny in the evening. The conversation went along these lines: (I'm 1965, John is 256, and DP is the detained person).

1965   'Now then pal, how are you doing?'

DP   'Ugh?'

1965   'I said now then, you, okay?'

DP   'Who me?'

1965   'Erm, yes, I already know who my teammate is. Can I have your name, please?'

DP   'My name? What do you want my name for?'

1965   'Cos you were driving the car.'

DP '   What car?'

256 'The car, the car in front.'

DP   'That's not my car.'

256 'Well whose car is it then?'

DP   'Eh?'

1965   'Right, let's start again. Name, please?'

DP '   My name?'

1965   'Ahh God! Please tell me your name.'

DP '   Eh?'

256 'What are you being stupid for?'

DP   'I wasn't driving.'

1965   'There's no one else in the car.'

DP	'Yeh, the driver's run off.'
256	'When? We've been behind you until we stopped you. I walked to the car, and you were in the driver's seat alone. The car's empty.'
DP	'What? Okay officers, I'm Imran Kha…. No, Imran Hussain.'
1965	'You were gonna say Khan then.'
DP	'NO! Imran Khan is my brother; he's disqualified from driving. We look alike, I'm carrying his driving licence.'

By this time, John and I are pissing ourselves in the car. We can see the cogs whirring around in his brain. He's trying the best he can to lie, but we know he couldn't even lie straight in bed. He won't be able to keep going much longer, pressured by John and I.

1965	'Okay Imran Khan/Hussain. How Old Are You?'
DP	"ME? Erm, 36.'
1965	'36! You don't look it. What's your birth date then?'
DP	'Who, me? What you want my date of birth for?'
256	'Because you were driving the car.'

DP	'What car? It's 03-05-76.'
256	'So how old does that make you?'
DP	'44!'

This could go on for hours if we wanted it to, but it had got to where we decided we needed to crack on. I break out the fingerprint device and scan his fingers. Lo and behold, it comes back as a disqualified driver. Imran Khan, born 03-05-2004. Now we must start all over again.

DP	'No officer, they're not my fingerprints. They must have been stolen by someone else, and they've used them. It's a setup.'

The technology in the cars now enables us to bring up a person's driving licence and all the details, including a photo. Yet, they can have missing ears, scars across their faces, a devil tattoo on their forehead, and they still claim it's not them.

The downside to all this new technology is that it is isolating. Your normal day-to-day interaction, say with the control room, all disappears. I've gone full days where the only people I have talked to have been 'Billy Shit Bags'. Your life becomes influenced by the negative crap from negative people; often calling you negative names. You put on a brave face; you've heard it all before. It doesn't bother me, pal, I say in my head. But of course, it does, with no one to speak to; you ask yourself if you really are a twat. 'Should I be catching the real criminals? Was I really bullied at school? Does anyone love me?'

As human beings, we grow and develop through our interaction with others. We need cuddles, a handshake, to chat and above all, to be loved. It comes with the territory. We are social beings who thrive on our communication with others. Take that away and we think things we would never normally think. Isolation goes against human nature. It's a big issue with the COVID-19 pandemic we are currently facing. People are becoming isolated and suffering from mental illness because of it. Even children are becoming stressed at not being able to see their friends. We need human company.

Office workers, shop assistants and hoteliers are constantly talking to people and chatting positively. It's good for the soul. Now, take police officers and fast responding paramedics attending job after job, where they're dealing with the negative aspects of life. It must play on their minds and emotions; I know it did mine. As computers get smaller and smaller, their memories get bigger and bigger. We get increasingly quicker answers. Information by the ton is fed to us, but this is sterile; it lacks emotion, love or empathy.

My illness has made me look at life differently and allowed me to know myself better, to grow in a more positive way. And, whilst I would never be a bible basher, I think God put us on this earth for a reason. Even if it's simply just to help someone else have a more positive life. I do hope my books are doing this and helping people with their own journey.

One thing I've realised is that being at home, life seems to have slowed down. It ran at such a fast pace before. I think that's true for so many people. Chasing criminals down leaves little time for thinking or planning. You get home and just want to go to sleep. The strain of the day is too heavy to carry. I read somewhere that facing a constant barrage of negativity can damage your health in so many ways. The changes which take place in the mental state upset your body's hormone balance and reduce the chemicals in the brain that bring happiness. It also damages the immune system and can lead to premature death. I don't want to think about that one, I've enough challenges going on right now.

If I look at the change in car crime, it's a prime example of how crime patterns have changed massively. In 2001, just 19 years ago, cars were stolen as they are now, but with several differences. 'Twoc-ing' - (Taking without consent), vehicle theft and fights were the main crimes. Cars were stolen to go joyriding in and then just abandoned. It was simple; you had your old cars, Y registration vehicles, plus older cars like the Cavaliers, Nova's, and Toyota Corollas, which were so easy to break into and hot wire or barrel the ignition. To secure such vehicles, you either had to buy a manufacturer proved 'Thatcham alarm,' or use a 90's style 'Stop lock.' Now all that security is included in the car's manufacture.

Back then you simply had to walk alongside the car and pop it open with a screwdriver, or half a tennis ball. You could then hot wire it within two minutes, which was so easy to do, or just thrust a screwdriver into the barrel and you were off. Most of the other crimes in Keighley were public order infringements, 'Friday and Saturday fight night,' we called it, brawling, house fights, pub fights and street fights. Mostly it was what you would class as bare-knuckle stuff. Sure, there were burglaries as well, plus drug taking, but car theft and public order incidents were the Chief's priority.

Without the technology to trace driving licences, vehicle insurance, and only having a very basic tracker unit to find cars, you just had used your copper's nose, but today, apart from your dental records, I pretty know everything there is to know about you, from the touch of a button. It just felt so much easier then, and it felt like the jobs were simple too.

Fast forward to 2020 and the change is unbelievable. The major things happening now are 'County Line' drug offences. So, where there would be your petty drug dealer on his local patch, now many dealers are going across counties and spreading out. They get young lads with no previous convictions involved, to go into a different county and deal the drugs. If we stop them, they aren't known, they're invisible. They're not on any criminal register and can just blend into the crowd. If they were doing it in the Bradford and Keighley District, they would be known and would be on our radar. For the criminals higher in the food chain, the money is phenomenal.

If you look at the crime 'Hanoi burglaries,' or 'two-in-one burglary,' as we call it, there is a break in at your house, with the explicit purpose of obtaining car keys and stealing your car. The name 'Hanoi Burglary' came from the code name of the first police operation targeting the method. In theory, the key's signal should no longer reach the car when the driver moves away, making it impossible to unlock the car. That type of burglary has now boomed.

The price of the car, and the insurance on the car, were not costly in the early 2000s. But from 2010 onwards, it boomed, and it's been the same ever since. The reason is that they now see that they can get more for the car second-hand than dumping it somewhere down a back alley. Say, for example, you are looking at a Golf R. The engine alone could be worth five to ten grand, a couple of grand for the seats and interior, a thousand pounds for the wheels, so cars are being stolen to order rather than just picked up and used for joyriding.

Criminals have realised that there is a market for stolen cars. They'll still 'rag it around,' but then they will sell it for parts on places like e-Bay. There might be a ten-grand engine for sale at five grand on one of these sites. As an officer you've HPI'd it, it's not illegal, and it's not shown as stolen. All the documents check out. It's easy to get a fraudulent document now; you can even print them off certain websites. What they do is steal a Golf R in blue that matches a certain spec. They hire a Golf R with the same spec from a hire car company, change and swap the engines, wheels and any other parts they can sell, and it's now the hire car that's driving around with the stolen parts on. All the hire car's stolen parts are then sold as legal parts and never traced or identified as stolen; the hire company doesn't know what's happened.

The higher powered, or more limited edition of the car, the more 'shit bags will pay. We were speaking to burglars who could be paid from three hundred to three thousand pounds for each car. Now if you're doing three cars a night, you're earning a hell of a good living. So, the way to break into houses became more creative. If these criminals used as much inventiveness in a normal job, they would become successful entrepreneurs. Years ago, they would just try your door handle to see if your door was open. Now they will just snap your lock off with some pliers and get in that way. They also use fishing rods to hook your keys off your side stand by your front door. You wouldn't know, you would be happily cooking dinner, singing away; oblivious to what was happening just feet away from you at your own front door.

It would be four hours later when I called you, asking if you know where your car is. You'd say, 'outside my house officer.' I'd tell you it had just been used in an armed robbery in Chapeltown, Leeds; made off at high speed and crashed through a wall. I remember one time when a car was reported stolen at 7pm, and by 9pm we found it in a back street in Bradford. It was standing on blocks with everything stripped. All that they had left was the shell. They had literally taken the interior, the roof lining, the electric cabling, everything you could take off a car had gone. Stripped bare in two hours; someone had even nicked the doors. We used to say if your car's not been found in five hours, it's on a shipping container to Southern Ireland or Dubai, never to be seen again.

Then the crimes got more inventive. Criminals would use blow torches to melt the handle and its mechanism so it would just open. It was that simple. Then, when it got to where cars were keyless, they would get a scanner and scan the code from your key, send it to your car and it would start; simple as that. You are in bed, sleeping soundly. The only time you're aware of your loss is if I come knocking at your door, or next day when you are ready to go to work.

One of the key issues police face today is the amount of information out there for all to see at the touch of a button. It's all available online, you can go on the internet and buy a scanner reader, tracker blocker, car key reader and more. There's also the black web, the internet criminals use. where you can buy absolutely anything. But don't forget, the Police, and Intelligence Services can still track people and criminals. They can track us all at GCHQ. They can find out your IP address and be at your house in ten minutes, there are ways and means. With certain cars, if you lose your keys or someone steals them, replacements must be bought from

Germany from the primary dealers. Some garages have car key readers, when you put your key in they can scan it to bring up who owns the car, where you live, registration and the chassis number. If we were doing a house search, we could go to a house and find several stolen car keys, we could then scan them to find out who the key belongs to, etc.

Stealing or copying car keys is big business, leading the criminals to the location of the car that they want. Take your high-end cars; you could turn over ten grand a night as a car thief because they'll pay you as much as two grand a key. They use anonymous drivers - 'Mr Bloggs' is a 'no mark,' who has no record, or criminal history. The mastermind then tells Mr Bloggs, 'I'll pay you three hundred quid to drive this car from A to B on cloned plates.' Chances are he won't get stopped, because the car won't be reported stolen until the following morning, and he will have already dropped it off and walked away.'

The sticky time is if it's been a 'Hanoi burglary' and the crime is reported straight away. We would know if you were making your way back from, say, Harrogate to Bradford. First thing we would do is find out what cameras are on the route. We would place units in several locations with ANPR and wait for you to drive past. From experience, we know the routes you are taking, and we can track what you are doing. If it's Joe Bloggs driving it when it's stopped, they will arrest him for the burglary, but only prosecute him for handling stolen goods. He'd simply say that someone paid him to drive it to a location. They would then kick him out with a slap on the wrists, maybe even a caution at most.

Burglaries have got more violent now and threats of violence are used more than ever before. I know of someone attacked on a forecourt with a machete for his car keys. This was in broad daylight. They started hacking away, carving him up like a piece of meat. Imagine the terror that the car owner felt. If they will do that in the daytime in a public place, what will they do at night-time in your house? Can you imagine the fear, if you hear something at 3 a.m., and you get to the top of your stairs and face somebody ready to hack you up, telling you they are going to kill you, then rape your wife and murder your kids unless you throw your car keys down. What's the first thing you will do?

There have been families who have been 'bare knuckle boxers,' or just complete 'bad asses,' who shout back from the top of the stairs, 'come and fucking get 'em.' What do you do? You have an unstoppable force versus an immovable object! Something has got to give. I'll tell you of one incident that I'll never forget. The criminals had got the wrong address; someone had left a high-powered car parked outside their neighbour's house. So, burglars entered the house, while a family function was taking place, and the residents faced four masked intruders carrying axes and machetes. They walked straight in and the first thing they did was hack one bloke, a 20-year-old. They lacerated his arm and nearly cut his hand off. Next, they hacked dad and screamed, 'give us the fucking car keys now.' The family was confused, asking 'what car keys?' Mum was cooking in the kitchen, unaware of events. In her hand she had a ten-inch carving knife to help prepare the evening meal. She shouted, 'tea's ready in ten, what do you want with it?' She heard no reply so walked into the front room, knife still in her hand. Mum then saw a bloke standing there with a machete, and mask on, and plunged the knife deep into his chest.

They turned and ran outside. 'Shit bag one' still had the knife embedded in his chest. The police then issued an intelligence bulletin to every hospital in England. It was clear that he needed urgent medical attention, or he'd die of his injuries. They found him in a caravan park around eight days later. He was just holding on, still sitting there with the knife in his chest, but he'd wrapped industrial tape around it. It was going septic and poisoning him. It got to the point where he had to ring '999' for an ambulance to assist him. Nothing happened to the wife, they didn't charge her with any offences; she had just reacted to the situation. But the level of violence and just down right cheek to secure a car key was horrific.

In their minds, all they know is that the car is being stolen to order and is worth a lot of money to them. If some guy in Dubai says I want a flash car in 'stone grey,' and I'll pay you ten grand to get it for me, what do they do? They're 'shit bags,' they will do anything to get it. The gangs engaged in such actions are real criminals and they're making money hand over fist. These aren't simple 'old school' car thieves; these are major gangs, organised and violent. People don't understand when they put pictures of their classy, expensive new car on Facebook or Instagram. It's like waving a red flag. It's easy to find out where people live today.

When we catch the car thieves, they will try anything to get rid of their phones. They know that on one phone they may have the details of fifteen unique addresses, cars, and whether the houses are occupied, lined up for that night's work. They move from one to another, stealing cars on demand. In most cases, the car ends up in Bradford. The planning and execution of these thefts is unbelievable. They watch the houses and track the owner's movements, to work out the best time to strike.

To give an example, we once had a very high powered X5 parked in Apperley Bridge train station. A witness phoned, saying that there were some people hanging around a car, and they didn't look like they could afford an eighty-thousand-pound car; they looked shifty. We made enquiries, and the car belonged to a well-known jeweller who was very wealthy. When a police officer got there and looked under the car, the suspects had put a tracker on it. All they were going to do was track the car to its home address and then do the robbery there. They are always three to four steps in front. Now, you think, 'if that man hadn't rung up.... that jeweller and his family could have been robbed, beaten and left emotionally damaged for life'.

In 2001 you only had to be one step ahead of the culprits, but now you must be four steps in front to keep up. Instead of attending repeated burglaries and being reactive, you must look at the routes they will take and know which way they are travelling back and forth and become proactive. That way you can guarantee that when you receive the next call informing you of a burglary you will already have anticipated the route and will be lying in wait.

There's also a lot of fraud goes on with such crimes. On one occasion the gang had an address somewhere and had used it to purchase a new Audi car. Now Audi has its own fraudulent finance team so we can phone them and say, 'they have used this car for x, y, z' and they will withdraw it, so we are cutting a burglar's wheels off. On the job we were dealing with, we went to the address where this Audi had been registered. It was a massive house in a posh area, something that you wouldn't look twice at, but the gates had been chained up and the hedges and bushes were all overgrown. When you looked at the house from the garden, the householders had used emulsion paint on all the windows so we couldn't see in. When we spoke to the neighbours, they told us that no one had lived there for ten years.

We're talking about a five hundred thousand pounds house here, not some shitty hovel in a dangerous area. This is a luxury house in a residential area, but we couldn't get, or speak, to the occupants. One of my oppos, a petite girl, squeezed through the railings and went around the back to the door. When she looked down on the floor, she could see envelopes from the passport office. When we checked on the police systems, we could see there were around sixty to seventy Asian males, all registered at this address. So, it was a fraudulent address for people to take finance out on cars using fake passports.

A simple job then led to a massive criminal organisation, fraudulently acquiring millions of pounds worth of high-powered cars on finance. The cars were registered and sent to the address, where they put false plates on a matching legitimate car. If they were stopped, all the illegally bought cars would be identified as legitimate. So, the main player could have four Audi RS6's at the back of his house, all in the same colour, all the same registration, all insured to him. The only way we could apprehend him is if one left the Bradford area. Some would be so stupid; they would lend one car to a friend, who drove it to Manchester, while the other was driving around Bradford. Both drove through speed cameras, simultaneously.

So, back in the early 2000s, attending nightclub fights etc. was the norm, but that's almost gone. Criminals don't go to nightclubs; it just doesn't happen now, they're too busy earning money. Now the night scene is just for kids and students. Criminals are getting technical, phoning your granny to cheat her out of her money, or doing 'Air B & B' fraudulent websites to con money from holidaymakers who turn up and find there is no accommodation.

The internet has been brilliant in some ways, but it's also left a massive wake of cheated people behind it. I honestly don't know why, when we can track IP addresses and get all sorts of personal information from the net, that car manufacturers can't simply fit a tracker into cars. We would know where any car was as a result; it would reduce insurance costs and car thefts. Once I was in a certain manufacturer's showroom and they said to me, 'we don't put them in because if we did, we wouldn't sell many cars, would we?' Can you believe that? But what they mean is, when a car gets stolen, the owner collects the insurance money and must go back into the showroom to buy another car.

Another fundamental difference now is how parents react to involvement with the police compared with 2001. Then, I used to love taking kids back to their parents when they broke the law. They either got a good bollocking or were grounded and made to apologise. There were only a few, and it was more the wealthier parents who would deny that their child had done anything wrong. It would always be someone else's kid's fault and wasn't their child. I would get 'My son wouldn't do that, you're wrong.' 'Well, they would, and they have,' I'd reply. 'We have caught him smashing windows in a church.' But the more respectable and hard working the family, the more they would be furious that their loved one had brought police to their door.

Other people are upset and disgusted. The kids are in tears, as they know what they have done. We've also taken kids back to more deprived areas, you know the place, where even granny has served time, dads just got out of nick on bail and it's like, 'Fuck off, don't lie about my son. Get out of my house.' What the police say is just falling on deaf ears, they don't care. The kid is just following their example.

There have been cases where we've been ragged around by 15-year-old kids who are bigger than we are. They were on crack or heroin and off their heads. They've been using steroids since they were 13; they know how to handle knives and they are just fucking dangerous people. We have a saying that we deal with someone on their level, but sometimes we can't do that, we need to escalate the level to take charge of the situation. We must physically fold them into the car whilst they're shouting, 'Fuck you, copper.' It's then, when you're hands-on, they realise, 'shit, this copper's not messing about.' Sometimes we must show them we are in control.

Today, they treat us with utter disrespect. They find it funny to rag a bobby, spit and lash out. I have had to change the way I police. Now I'll stare at them with a look that says, 'Don't fuck me about, I'll not stand for any shit.' Sometimes it's a stand-off, they want to show-off in front of their mates, be the big man. I'm trying to bring order to a dangerous situation that could kick-off. I must revert to using their own language to make them understand, I'm not kidding or messing about, I'm too old for that shit; push me and I'll make an example of them in front of their gang.

If it was pissing down with rain, I would keep him on the pavement, with my knee on his back, under control. I may get wet through, but I'm showing his pals what will happen if they try to butt in or push the boundaries. The next time I have them in my car, they will put their hands out when told to, and not give me a 'Fuck you pig' response. Word soon gets around; and someone has it on camera and 'You Tube' before you can say boo. It shows them up in front of their mates, and the rest of them realise this is a copper they can't piss about with. If the parents backed us up when their kids got into trouble, our job would be so much easier.

I'll give you an example of one guy I knew. It didn't matter what you said, his grandparents wouldn't have it. If someone said to them. 'I heard your grandson got locked up for burglary.' They would say, 'No, no, he didn't do it. It wasn't burglary. He was round the back of someone's house, collecting scrap. I don't know why they locked him up because he didn't do that.' Well, come on. You can't just lock someone up for burglary unless you have proof. The custody sergeant would throw it straight out. If you locked him up for burglary and didn't give the correct grounds, or it wasn't the right offence for what you had locked him up for, the custody sergeant wouldn't accept it.

Ironically, the witness to the burglary was a copper, who had phoned, saying 'the suspect is round the back of this house trying to break in,' but his family still wouldn't have it. Another time they locked him up for stealing a motorcycle. That time they said that he hadn't stolen it, he had found it in the woods; even though the suspect had been seen riding the motorcycle. Every time he got locked up, the family would buy him a steak dinner when he got out, as they felt like he was being wronged. They would tell everybody that the police were against him for no reason. No, we weren't against him, he was a criminal and a thieving shit.

It got to the stage where once he was in a pool car; he made off from the police and was chased. The chase finished when he rammed someone; he got out and ran off but left his provisional driving licence at the scene. The officer pursuing him knew who he was, but he denied it. The family then turned around and said it was the police's fault. It wasn't him; someone had stolen his driving licence. They wouldn't have it that their son and grandson was just a 'bad egg.' If they are rewarding him with steak and fuelling him with praise, then he will feel like he can do as he wants.

That's where things have changed, I used to see parents smacking their kids around their heads if they did anything wrong. Now it's, 'Have you got it on your phone? Cos if you've touched my son, I'm going to do you. Have you got any proof it's him?' You can tell them you got him out of the seat of the stolen car, and they will ask for proof you did that.

They then go into prison and come out wiser than when they went in. Criminals now 'Facebook' live crimes as they're happening. They get instant kudos; Mr 'Bad Ass' within minutes. Now, they don't even have to go to each other's houses. They have things like Zoom, they can organise all sorts without going out of the house. Parents aren't aware of what they are doing when they are in their bedrooms using the internet half the night. They're learning all sorts from programmes and online videos; they can even learn how to steal a car on 'YouTube.'

One example I can give that really pissed me off is when I was on the Police Interceptors. Criminals quickly recognised from another 'reality police programme,' called 'Traffic Cops,' that when a pursuit got too dangerous, we had to abort. What did they do? As soon as we were closing in, they started driving where they could endanger others, so we had to abort. Now it has all changed in our favour. The police pursuit policy says that we can follow. I have to say that I don't think we should have had to give our tactics away. Criminals shouldn't know our likely responses. We should have the full backing of the force in that. Some revealed tactical information has helped criminals learn more about what we do to catch them.

In America they have what's called the PIT manoeuvre, 'Police Intervention Tactics.' So, they will go behind a car and PIT it, spin it. We aren't taught that in our police, but if you need to end a pursuit, you will use it. It has involved me in a few jobs where I've been told, 'You will not let this car get away. Do not let it get to Bradford or the City centre.' So, I will put it to bed in a safe, controlled manner.

I have a massive scar all the way down my finger on my left hand. It resulted from a burglary in Baildon. I got behind this car; conditions were bad, and I was pursuing it alone. It went all the way around Shipley, towards Bradford, and came back on Canal Road. The pursuit was along a minor road; I knew the stolen car must do a hard right to come back on itself. It was speeding down the road, when it anchored on its brakes, and went wide. I knew what he was trying to do, he was heading for Crag Road, so I asked myself 'how long can I let this pursuit go on for?' I knew that eventually one of us was going to be killed or badly injured. I could see now that a firearms car was on its way, closing in behind me. We were on a road where, if the escaping car continued, he had nowhere to go. On one side was a big drop, with a large, grassed area on the other. I thought 'fuck this,' and as he spun around in front of me, I P.I.T manoeuvred him. There wasn't much contact made on my car, but he went into a 180 degree spin. The firearms car blocked the front of the bandit vehicle, as both his and my police car travelled up the grassy embankment and came to a stop.

I left my car, smashed his passenger's side window and reached through in order to rag him out of the car. On doing so, the driver ran my hand around the shards of glass still stuck in the door, ripping my fingers to bits. I had bits of glass in my fingers and flaps of skin hanging off.

When I returned to the nick, I reported the reclaimed stolen car, and the thief was about to be sent down. This is when the questions began. 'Should you have really done that? If you hadn't got other units backing you up, shouldn't you have aborted?' All of this is being put out over the media. Should they know what my tactics are? My sergeant backs me and I'm proud. An officer must use judgement in these situations, but should the public be aware of what I'm using from my arsenal?

We are accountable for everything, must answer for everything, and the criminals know it. We have lost the respect we had when I first started in the force. One problem, and they may criticise me for saying this, but I really believe that they have now made the police force the 'Jack-of-all-trades'. People phone into the control room for the most stupid things. 'I've missed my last bus home. Can you send a car to take me? If you can't I'm going to hurt myself.' Sounds crazy, but they introduced a process whereby we had to answer all calls. We would have to send a unit to make sure that the caller was safe. So instead of being there just to prevent and deal with crime, we became fall guys who dealt with a wide range of public issues.

The result of being there for everybody and everything is that we don't get to where we want to be, and then we are slated for that. This is a controversial example. The Yorkshire Ripper died recently. The first thing West Yorkshire Police did was to come out and apologise to all his victims. I'm 'fucked off,' and I'm thinking, 'why do you have to apologise for what the police did 35 years ago?' You need to be quiet, let the families move on now he's gone, let them be at peace. We didn't have the technology then; we didn't have the science we do now, officers did the best they could. You wouldn't get a NASA spokesperson coming out and apologising for not getting a man on the moon sooner. If a serial killer went on for that length of time today, without being caught, then apologise.

Nowadays every single complaint made is investigated, even if we know it's nonsense. When I was in Keighley, we had a 'help desk' in the town centre. The number of complaints we got against bobbies every Friday and Saturday was unbelievable. They'd stagger in, 'pissed,' waving their arms around and it would be: 'Hey, I want to complain about Ben Pearson.' 'Okay, what do you want to complain about?' 'Err not a clue, I just want to complain.' So, we moved the 'help desk' down the road. How many complaints did we get then on a weekend? Fuck all, because they weren't arsed to walk down the road to the police station, because it was nowhere near the kebab shop.

We would then get them ringing up saying, 'I want to make a complaint.' They would be told to come down to the police station, but again they couldn't be arsed to make the journey. Now, they can do it online or over the phone. They don't have to lodge a complaint as in 2001. It's so easy for them now. They can do it sitting in their beds watching their relatives on Jeremy Kyle.

I remember once, I had a bit of a vendetta against this lad because he was always driving without insurance. When he saw me, he would make off, do two lefts and a right and then dump the car. I'd get there, and he'd be standing against the side of his car, but because I didn't stop him driving, we couldn't convict him. One day I got behind his car and it made off. I found it behind the back of his house in an alleyway. His brother came out, a lad about 17, the other was 21. He said to me. 'Fuck off, you white copper bastard,' then threw a punch at me. I hit him; he went down like a sack of shit. I pinned his arms behind his back and locked him up.

The older one then came out effing and jeffing, and we seized his car. By the time I'd got to the nick, he'd phoned in. 'I was racist, I'd called him a Paki bastard. He's just locked my brother up and broke his arm. I want to put in a complaint.' By this time, I've booked his brother into the cells, he's apologised for accusing a police officer of being racist, apologised for swinging a punch at a police officer and he's declared that he has no injuries and there is nothing wrong. His sibling is still upholding the complaint even though his uninjured brother is in the cells apologising. He gets a fixed penalty ticket for public order, and he's kicked out.

The complaint is still running. 'Well Ben, you've broken this lad's arm, we have to run it.' I'm thinking, 'this is shit, go look at the custody record, ask the custody sergeant. He's got no injuries.' Still, they are running it to make sure I'm not racist. This was before body cameras or when cars had cctv. I'm getting so annoyed, no one seems to listen to me. 'Just check it out, look at the record.' This wouldn't have happened before, but they are so scared of the racist card and criminals know it. They have no respect for the truth. Now, even though it was unfounded, it went on my file that he had made a complaint against me. It stains my record for a lie that wasn't proved, and with clear evidence to the contrary.

The police are an easy target for blame now. Accountability has become misunderstood and used against us rather than to support us. We have less respect for ourselves, the organisation has less respect, so the public has less respect. We've become a public apology for everything.

Do I wish we were back in the days of 'Heartbeat'? With some things, yes. The force needs to gain back the respect it once had and stop apologising for doing our job the best we can. There is a short 'spoof' video uploaded on Facebook where a Scottish Chief Constable must apologise to everybody, including the squirrels, for cutting down trees. He's bald, and finally gives apologies for his appearance possibly offending bald men. Yes, it's funny, and it's far-fetched, but its message is real.

Chapter 3 - Let's Talk Duty

Oh, how I hated KPI's, the little tick sheets they would send around the office. These record your work hours for your supervisor. I used to get pissed off because I would spend an hour helping some poor old lady who was lost to get home. It would make me feel good.

Back in the office it would count for nothing, but they would give my teammate, who had issued two tickets in that time, ticks for documenting incidents. It left me looking like I was a real lazy prat, even though I had used my time to help a vulnerable member of the public.

Being on duty is not all rushing from one crime scene to another. There are nights when it is relatively quiet. On such nights, it felt like everyone had taken sick leave and decided they couldn't be arsed to go out. I would then be quizzed because I hadn't been able to get any results. Surely, that should be a good thing though, no active burglars, no stolen cars. But, no, I was seen as somehow lacking. I would have appreciated being praised for nothing happening on my patch, not questioned.

I learned to be crafty; I used to keep a little green book in the back of my traffic folder. It contained the phone numbers of people I had arrested and who had freely given them, I may add. Mainly, they were those I dealt with regularly, issuing warrants every other month. When I knew I was down on figures, I would check who hadn't turned up to court. There would always be one who hadn't.

I would then contact them up and tell them they could either answer the door to me and come quietly or face the 'big red key' at 4am. I would let them sit in the front of the car with me, so they didn't lose respect. I would even stop at the garage to get them some Diet Coke and a packet of crisps when they were on the 'H plan diet.' I knew it would top them up before they hit the cells for the night; some even welcomed the 5-star accommodation, a room with a view and quality B & B.

There was this one 'meat head' in Keighley, well respected among the criminal fraternity and feared by many. Arriving at his door, I would knock and shout, 'It's Ben, there's another warrant in your name.' 'Fuck you, go get some backup, you fucking piggy bastard,' he would shout back. I would continue to explain to him he could come, and I would get him some 'pickled onion Monster Munch' and a 'Twix,' or whatever he wanted. He would open the door and come out smiling.

Covered in tattoos and scars from his many altercations, he had to have the last word. He would say. 'I'm only coming because I want a Mars Bar.' Happy and content at the way I was dealing with him, a Mars Bar was a small price to pay for one more KPI.

Not every pickup goes my way. There was the time I came across one of my regulars who had become homeless. I had seen him around Keighley Centre, harassing members of the public. He was being a pain and was drunk on 40% proof cider. He stank like old socks.

I knew there was a warrant out for him, but because of the state he was in, most had just left him alone. I thought, 'Fuck it.' There was nothing else going on, so I spoke to my smelly friend. He responded by slurring and using every profanity he could think of, so I arrested him.

It was only a shop-lifting warrant, so it was more than likely they would release him on bail the same day. As I stuck him in my car, I noticed he smelled horrible. I put the windows down and got to Keighley nick sharpish. Once booked in, I had to search him to make sure he had no offensive weapons or drugs on him. Now I know that I should have done that before I put him in the car, but it was in the days when we didn't wear stab vests, and there wasn't the violence towards the police that there is today.

I went through the procedure. 'Is there anything on you that could hurt myself or my colleague?' He said nothing. I just got a drunken stare and slight wobble. I got to my knees and patted him down. Holding my nose because of the stink. It was the odour that makes your mouth go dry and brings tears to your eyes.

As I ran my hands around his waistband, he says. 'Be careful, I've got a knife in my pant leg.' Immediately, I'm on guard. 'Hands on the counter,' I shout. He tells me it's down his right leg. On searching him I find a 4-to-5-inch hard object. It was straight and to the right of his sock. Confused by the shape, I pulled the object to the rear of his pant leg. He was wearing two pairs of pants and three pairs of socks; the lagging wasn't helping. He chuckled to himself as I rolled the object around in his pants. 'This is a strange, shaped knife,' I'm thinking to myself.

In one of my more stupid moments, I squeezed it. He let out a loud belly laugh. 'Got ya,' he shouted triumphantly. You guessed it. The now squidgy lump was a hardened shitty turd he'd had in his pants for three days; solidified in the cold air of the streets.

We marched him into his cell and gave him a clean pair of pants. For the next 30 minutes he banged loudly on his door, demanding dinner and a warm blanket, plus something to read. I got what he needed and opened the flap on his cell to pass them through. Two filthy, shit-laden arms came through towards my face. He had started a three-hour dirty protest, rubbing his crap everywhere he could in the room.

The public order unit arrived, wearing full riot gear covered with white 'SOCO suits.' Only then could we remove him from his cell. They then classed him as a 'Pol 1' prisoner, so I had to sit and supervise him for hours on end. The smell of his faeces was everywhere. This turned out to be the world's shittiest KPI arrest ever. I decided that my little book of numbers just wasn't worth it and stopped using it the very next day.

I'll never forget that lock-up, and the same goes for the first time that I was ever in a police car. Sam and responded to a 'blue light' job. I'm going back to 2002 now, when there was no such a thing as 'Sat-Nav'. You relied on the good old A to Z map book. I'd never been in a car that was 'blue lighting', so you have to remember that it was a new experience at the time.

I fastened my seat belt and Sam hit the accelerator. I was just like a civilian in a police car. It was only a small vehicle compared to the ones we use now. An Astra 1.6, but I physically couldn't concentrate due to the speed. That wouldn't affect me now one bit; I'm well trained. But then, I struggled to even fasten the seat belt. I was trying to lean into the back of the car where my kit bag was. It contained my huge six cell mag light, now it would be a little three-inch LED torch. Then, there was my little unused ticket folder, back then if you gave one ticket out a week that was about it, now it's expected that you'll do around ten to fifty a week.

Sam floored the car; instant pure fear went through my entire body. I thought, 'fucking hell, wow...look at this.' I was in a car with an officer who was driving and in complete control, whilst I was anything but. She told me the address, and to look for an American sounding name. There was I, who couldn't spell for toffee, trying to look at the A to Z whilst she's flying up this street at 70mph. I had a tiny interior light to help me see and read. I bluffed, telling my tutor I couldn't find it, embarrassed that I couldn't read properly in that situation.

Thankfully, she knew the area, and she found the address. You understand that, even on foot patrol, you had a side pouch on your belt with an A to Z inside. I used to dread somebody coming up and asking if I knew where somewhere was. Now, of course I would know, but then it was pure embarrassment. My heads like a 'Sat Nav' now, I know all the areas I worked in. I also knew all the motorway networks. In my last few years, I could tell you how to get to any of them without a 'Sat Nav' or old school 'A to Z.'

At the time, all I could hear was a whirring sound from the rotary lights on the roof. We had these police radios like blocks of concrete, like that guy on telly who has the big phone he carries around. Everything we had was big then. It hindered all your movements and getting out of the car at speed was just a joke. I found it really hard to manage the map; I was experiencing my first 'blue light' run, breaking the law legally. The first time you do it, it's shit scary. I used to love it when years later probationers came out with me. I didn't want to scare them, but when you are flying through traffic and they sit there saying, 'Jesus, how do you do this?' you realise just how good you have become over the years.

You have total admiration for real drivers. They are multi-tasking in a way that's incredible. Scanning the road, watching where pedestrians are, listening to their radio, talking to their oppos. You can't say 'be quiet, I'm concentrating.' It's on a level you can't understand unless you have done it.

I'm worried that now I wouldn't be able to do it; in fact, I know I couldn't. Even then I had reading and writing challenges, and massive low confidence issues. If an e-mail came out about a new law, people would just remember it and I couldn't. It's common knowledge that as a police officer you must keep up with the law and I found I wasn't. It was moving faster than I could take it in.

I realised I would really struggle with paperwork, whereas I excelled at my driving. Today, everything is computerised, and it takes only an hour or two at most to get paperwork done. There are spell checks, grammar prompts and a host of helpful stuff, but then it was five hours of hard work handwriting and filing. My dyslexia caused me some genuine problems.

I found I wouldn't want to go to any job where I had to take a big, lengthy statement or where I had to bag a lot of exhibits up. That would involve too much writing for me to do. I saw others bypassing me because they were much quicker. I even questioned whether police work was for me; should I find something else to do?

I once had to take a statement. I was out with Sam and the suspect had a bomber jacket on. I spelt bomber, bomer. Sam asked me what I was doing in front of the complainant. She pointed out how you spell it correctly. She needed to because it must be accurate there and then. They must initialise any error so you can't change it afterwards. It's an official statement, a legal document.

I recall going red, and every single word I tried to spell got worse and worse. She took me to the side and told me how bad it was and what I was doing wrong. There were no dyslexia aids like now; it was just getting on with it and writing. I would structure how I wrote in my head. I would use simple words to avoid all big ones.

The handheld computers or laptops we now take with us to jobs, have really made things easier, especially for people like me. Different coloured screens and bigger words protect you from the glare. One problem I had when driving, was approaching road signs at a fast speed; if I stared at them the letters would move, A's and E's would become mixed. So, A330 might read AEEO to me. Due to this I had to study maps for hours on end. I only passed my advanced driving courses by having knowledge of the roads and locations, rather than knowledge of the signs.

It is strange though when you're a traffic cop. Most officers will tell you that the principal thing they deal with are pursuits, 'fatals' and collisions. You automatically think it's always humans, but that's not always the case. Many of what we deal with are more of the four-legged variety. Some officers would argue that we should concentrate on what we are there for; others see it as part of the job.

The reality is often far from what we should or shouldn't be dealing with. It's down to the person in the control room who sees the word road or carriageway in the incident report, and immediately it's 'traffics' job. 'Send it to Ben, he can deal with this.' Ben, who is alone in his traffic car and finds himself en route to deal with six large horses walking up and down the road. Am I to lasso them, round them up, like in the Wild West? Ride them, one by one, to safety? I'm single-crewed, what do I know about bloody horses?

Ducks, swans, rabbits, lots of rabbits; I've dealt with them all: deer, hedgehogs, sheep, a bull, cats, dogs and pigeons, those little flying rodents that like to go about in gangs. I recall one incident when, as young beat cop in Keighley, they partnered me with a great oppo called James. It would have been around 2004. Just as a long night shift was ending, we got a call over the radio. James shouted, 'Hotel Delta 1,' to show we were on it.

Off we went, flying through the streets to the emergency, logged at 4.45am with the sun just rising. Then I saw them, scrounging in the middle of the road, bloody pigeons. The last customers to feed from 'Barry and Scott's Donner Kebab' at 3am, had thrown their remnants in the street on their way home from some nightclub. Great, but we were travelling at a speed of 60 to 70 mph. James was frantically beeping the old R reg Vauxhall Astra horn and flashing his headlights.

The little shits wouldn't give up their dirty meat with chilli and garlic sauce; they continued to stuff themselves. We manoeuvred to avoid hitting them, but the chief honcho decided differently, he signalled the charge, and we now faced an army of them flying directly at the car. Now, anyone who has observed pigeons knows they leave it until the last minute before taking to the wing. 'Bang,' an explosion of feathers and dust crossed the windscreen. We looked for bodies in the road; there were none. How they escaped annihilation was a miracle, but they did. We were pleased, of course. I mean who wants to mow down a brood of starving pigeons?

Pigeons have nothing on Kamikaze rabbits. We would be up on Baildon Moor, and they would just randomly run out in front of our car. They had a strange way of killing themselves. They would hear and see us coming at high speed, but instead of turning away from the danger, they would run straight at us. 'Bang,' we would pull to a stop, look under the car and see nothing. How they escaped death I can't say, but they did. Maybe they were hitching a lift, hanging onto the undercarriage.

They say cats have nine lives; I believe it. We don't want to injure any poor animal, but they make it difficult for us not to. I recall an evening when me and my oppo, Baby Ben, were being filmed for 'Police Interceptors'. We were travelling down White Abbey Road at a great speed when suddenly a huge 'ginger tom' ran straight out in front of the car. We could do nothing to avoid it. 'Bang!' It sounded like we were hitting a lamp post. Ben skidded to a stop; we rushed out to check on the cat.

The front valance of the lower bumper had a tremendous crack in it. Fluff was stuck to it, but we couldn't find the cat. It really upset both of us at the thought of a badly injured animal laying somewhere. It affects us too; no one wants to hurt any living thing. Not being able to find it means that somewhere, there is an owner heartbroken at the disappearance of their pet. The same week, travelling towards Baildon Green, we saw a deer laying in the road; obviously hit by a car and left in pain. Such a majestic and beautiful creature, but in so much agony. Painful as it is, we knew the kindest thing to do was to put the animal down humanely.

Its back legs and spine were clearly broken. There was no way we were going to pull a ten stone deer into the back of the car. The animal was suffering and howling in pain, trying to move by dragging its shattered legs behind it. I really wanted to put my arms around it and say it's okay, but I knew to do that would scare it more than it was already.

We shouted over the radio that we needed help. Within seconds, a firearms car pulled up. Two massive officers pulled it into the grass and put it out of its misery. They lifted it into the rear of the X5 and drove away. Strange, I know, but I felt I had witnessed a murder. It's far easier to deal with a burglar than an animal, trust me.

Years ago, they sent me to Oxenhope. It was a fatal incident where a bull had trampled on a farmer in a field of cows, killing him. The bull had been protecting his ladies and saw the poor farmer as a threat. It was another situation where we couldn't remove the body because of the bull. So, firearms had to be called to shoot it. A sizeable crowd had gathered, and some were feeling sorry for the bull, but then realised that someone's family member was sprawled out dead in the field.

As much as it may be human nature to be curious and want to stop and ogle at accidents, people really need to stop and think of the victims and their families. They also want to ask themselves, as they take out their phone to get the gory picture, how they would feel if it were one of their family members? Perhaps they wouldn't be so keen to be amateur photographers then.

Once again, when I was with Baby Ben, we saw cars were swerving in the road and changing their course. We stop our car and out jumped Ben, shouting at the oncoming traffic to stop. There, crossing the road was mother duck followed by eight little ducklings, only three inches in height. It was like a scene from a Disney movie. Ben took his white traffic cap and became 'mother protector.' Gently, he lifted each duck and placed it in the hat before settling them over the stone wall, where their mother had already jumped over. When they were all safe, he came back to the car. The beaming smile on his face said it all.

I've not mentioned that other significant hazard, sheep. I can't count the number of times I've been parked on Hollins Hill, blocking the road with my car, trying to herd a flock of them back into the field they have escaped from. They will leap from any hole in the fence that they find. I'm there, 300 yards from my vehicle acting like a demented shepherd, screaming 'come bye' or 'away' - the sheep scattering in all directions, but I'm putting on the best comedy show the public has ever seen. They are pissing themselves laughing at me, beeping horns and waving.

Horses, no, I'm just not going there. A horse is a motorcycle with a brain. The only positive is that I don't have to take statements or exhibits from animals.

Handling animals may be tricky, but the most complicated calls that come through are the 'immediate' calls. The '999's where something untoward is happening as the call comes in, and we must respond within a certain time. The problem arises when the call handlers get further information that may change the status of the call. To give an example. I can rush to a scene to be informed by 'control' that a burglary is taking place. Then it becomes 'a man wearing a balaclava is knocking on the door asking for Sylvia.' I'm next told by 'control' that the man is drunk. It's then realised he is looking for Sylvia, and he's lost. He then pees in the street. Well, that's no burglar, is it? The 'pissed' man then phones Sylvia, who tells him he's on the wrong street. 'All units stand down...... cancel, cancel, cancel.'

A genuine issue is when you don't get to an 'immediate' in the required time. It then becomes a bollocking if an officer is missing too many targets. We must then justify why we missed arriving in the allotted time. The call handler is constantly juggling the information to give us as many details as possible. We must work in partnership, but sometimes we just rely on our own instincts.

I recall one incident where I received information that a man had left a broken-down Porsche on a bad bend with hazard warning lights on. I was then informed that someone was walking off across a field. Instantly, in my head, I knew something was wrong. It had to be a stolen car from a burglary. I shouted to 'control,' and it's now converted to an 'immediate job,' with all units required to swiftly attend. We found out that the car had been stolen in a burglary and crashed into a wall.

We also get the panic calls. A woman on her own reports she's heard someone in her house. The call handler is trying to get information from her, but she's so scared she can't remember anything. She says they have stolen her car, but she can't remember the registration. It's then up to the call handler to change tack and try to calm the women down before asking leading questions. Be calm, look out of the window, what do you see? You can imagine the state the woman is in; she's terrified, she could still be in danger, but doesn't know. It's important to reassure her, to help her to calm down, but also to enable us to get better information.

One call we got was to sort out a group of drunks spotted on CCTV. Bouncers had thrown them out of a nightclub for acting up inside. We got to the scene, pulled up, and there were all the revellers, eating their kebabs out on the street, still pissed up. The lad they had called us about was there making a fool of himself. He was covered in beer; after rolling around on the floor in the nightclub, there was a wet piss mark on his pants where he'd dribbled when he'd not got it out in time. He was complaining the door staff had been unfair and wanted them to be arrested.

We gave him two options. 'One, you either go to the kebab shop, then go home or two, just go home, but there's no way on earth you're getting back in'. Off he walked, head down, tail between his legs then, two minutes later he returned. He'd decided there'd been an injustice. I tell him, 'Fuck off and go away, I have told you to go away.' Then he got angry, and I told him again, 'last chance or you'll be arrested.' Off he went, only to return minutes later for another go at getting back into the club. Again, I repeated his options. I told him he was being a dick. He didn't like the way I spoke to him; he wanted to make a complaint. I told him, 'Go ahead, my collar number is on my shoulders.' I wouldn't deal with him anymore; he was pissed and acting like a moron. It then started. 'Fuck you, you don't know I'm pissed.' 'I know you're pissed because you are saying 'fuck you' to a police officer. You wouldn't do that in the daytime. What do you do for work?' 'I'm a solicitor,' came the reply.

'So, you're a solicitor and you're drunk in the street. They have thrown you out of a nightclub. Now don't you think you should be on your way home?'

Then he spat at me. If you know anything about me, you know I don't stand for that, so he's dragged with force to the floor, arms behind him, cuffs on, and I needed to get him into a van. I wouldn't put him in the car because I knew from experience that drunks will piss on, spit and kick the windows out. He's thrown in the back of a van. By the time we got him out, he'd pissed himself again and was in tears.
'It's all gone wrong, 'please let me go officer. I've not done anything wrong.'

His pants were wet through; he's laid in a cell. He might get some clean tracksuit bottoms. Next morning he's kicked out with a fine. Was it worth it? No, it wasn't. He's apologising for his foolish actions. Now, not only has he to explain to his boss why he's late for work, but that he'd also got a criminal conviction for being drunk and disorderly.

The problem with drunks is that they have this urge to speak, and even demand to be listened to. They want to engage with anyone who will listen to their bullshit. I don't want to engage; I just want them to get home. Some think they are above the law. I'll get comments like. 'Do you know who I am? I'm the Chief Executive of the Conservative Party. 'Well, I don't care who you are; you are breaking the law and you're looking stupid. 'I demand respect from you,' they shout. 'What, in the state you are in? Give over.' Next minute they are on the floor, either crying or kicking off. That said, men are nowhere near as violent as women.

Some women are as strong as men and will fight to the death. All we can do is go behind them and bear hug them. We don't get in the middle of the fight. They will think nothing of punching you, pulling hair or scratching your face. They can be so violently drunk. Clothes are being ripped off, heels thrown and little skimpy dresses up around their heads, it's unreal. It's best to leave them at it, and then clean up the aftermath.

They would end up with clumps of scalp in their hands, hair ripped out, bite marks. Blokes will normally throw five or six punches and then that's it, but not women. They'd scalp each other if they could. It's just horrible, a 5'4" blonde head butting everything in sight.

It's not all violent, there are the funny drunks; usually around Christmas and it's great to see. We've chased 'Smurfs' and 6ft high, 17 stone teddy bears down the road. There are people who've been locked up in banana suits, but I just want to see people who are happy. It's what most of us want. Happy drunks are pleasant drunks. When they come up just to talk to you and wish you a happy Christmas, its brilliant. No arguments or issues. Sadly, and increasingly, people seem to have a bitter taste in their mouths, and a chip on their shoulder for the police.

I remember one time when we were filming for 'Interceptors.' We came across a group of elderly men, drunk, standing next to a broken-down minibus. We pulled up to help and found out they were all from Newcastle. They were staying at Hollins Hall Hotel but were going the wrong way. They didn't know where they were going; they were all doctors and pissed as farts. They'd no sense of where they were or where they had been. It was then that one piped up. 'Can you imagine now if cameras were here? We'd all be on the

'Interceptors.' They were totally unaware that they were being filmed. That gives you an inkling of what it's like being a response cop.

What isn't realised is that a cop doesn't switch off. Once a cop, always a cop. You don't go home and leave the job behind. You're always on duty and aware of what is going on around you. Even though all you want to do at the end of your shift is get home, get into comfortable clothes and down a beer. You can't, you're always looking at what's there.

It would be great if you could just switch off when you've finished your work, but it's not so simple as that. You arrive home and notice immediately a car parked on your street that hasn't been there before. Is it one that's stolen and parked up to collect later?

You walk to your door, you're noticing the lock, are there any signs they have primed it? Is the gate shut at the side of the house? You hear a noise in the middle of the night. You can't ignore it; you are up and looking out at your car, and the street. You check your door. You don't want to, but you don't switch off and it's burning your energy all the time.

You can peacefully go shopping on a normal day, but not me. I can stand in a queue at Morrison's, but what am I seeing and thinking? I'm looking at people around me and my head is saying, burglar, rapist and thief. I know because some were on my briefing last night. I'm not on duty though, so I need to ignore it, not make eye contact, and make sure my kids are close next to me, safe and protected.

All coppers have a lot of baggage to carry around. They need to make many decisions extremely quickly, knowing all the time that one wrong decision can cost you your job or worse still, a life.

Chapter 4 - Just Nod and Smile

Confession time: I loved being on foot beat in the town centre, but I was jealous every time I heard of another officer who had gained a driver permit. I was gagging to get behind the wheel of a police car. I longed to be a police driver. Ever since I was a child, I have loved anything with an engine in it. A police car, however, was on another level. To be given permission to drive fast through red lights; to drive on the wrong side of bollards and get paid for it. It had to be one of the best jobs in the world. The buzz, the excitement, was second to none.

It seemed an eternity, and I was still waiting to start my driver training. Normally probationers complete their driving in the first two years, so at the end of your probation time you are a fully qualified Police Constable ready to specialise. Now, that's the theory, but not always the case.

By the middle of year two, I was becoming pissed off. I had asked and asked but continued to wait for my training. In 2002/2003, there were only a handful of police driving instructors. They either ran the standard or advanced courses. Added to that, they covered all divisions and departments in the force, alongside probationers coming in every six weeks. It had to be a minefield to sort out.

I didn't give a fuck any more about the complications. It was my turn; I deserved it. I'd waited long enough. But after months of waiting, I just switched off and gave up. I enjoyed being on the beat. I'd watched the new officers being run ragged and thought, bollocks to this. I'd rather walk, drink tea and have a chat with people. I'd years left to build my career, so why give myself the pressure? There was no rush.

Ironic as it was, that same day, I got back to the office after a steady walk around town, listening to my radio beep 'Hotel Delta 1'. Every division had a 'Hotel Delta 1' car. It was the car that got bummed, left, right and centre. It never ate and had lock- ups several times a day. We then had 'Hotel Delta 3', known as the farm car. It was the Haworth Village area car, attending fields and sheep. It just ate ice-creams, helped granny across the road car and give directions to tourists.

I was absolutely buzzing when I saw the e-mail from 'duties,' and my divisional training officer informed me I had my driving course coming up. I was also a little scared, but the idea of having my own police car sent my head into a spin. Soon, I would be the owner and driver of a 1998 R registration Vauxhall Astra. One working rotor light on the top, a flash-up 'police' sign, and a wheel trim missing; a very different prospect from the modern police car you see today.

The car I was getting was the 'loner car,' given to all first-time drivers. No self-respecting officer would be seen driving it, but to me, it was great. I didn't care. I wanted it; I needed my wheels, and no one was going to stop me.

So here I am, at driver training. The police are teaching me how to do things that my parents and civilian driving instructors have told me not to do. It's my first day, and I have travelled to a small village called Crofton, just outside

Wakefield. It is a lovely place, painted houses, quiet streets and a quaint little police station surrounded by trees. It didn't look much on arrival. You parked your personal car on the gravel at the side of the building. A gap in the trees led you to the main driveway and the hustle and bustle of the station.

Police cars were parked up, officers running around, and stern-faced instructors walking about. Inside the old house, dating back to the 1940s, were four converted bedrooms. Once separated into groups, they allocated us our room. My heart was racing, and I loved it. I felt I was at 'Brand's Hatch,' in the pits waiting for my formula one car to arrive.

Two officers and my instructor sat in the car with me. The bobbies, Nick and Dave, were a good laugh, and we bonded immediately. Initially, we just enjoyed a couple of drives. I spent the first couple of days getting to know the workings of the car. You had to get used to how it sounded with the siren and lights on. It's one thing to drive a normal car, but one with lights and the siren blaring changes the way some people behave.

We were still learner police drivers at that point, but members of the public didn't know that. They could panic on hearing the sirens and behave stupidly when they saw us approaching. They all drove three mph under the limit when they saw us. They all think they are excellent drivers, but they can't operate at the level of a trained police officer; nor should we expect them to.

As a police officer, you need to be very observant, plan your drive, and be in your car eight hours a day at speeds up to and over 150mph plus. There must be an awareness of the way pedestrians, horses and other cars react to you; the challenges faced if you go the wrong way around a roundabout or into the opposite carriageway. I can tell you that after 19 years in the job, I was still learning every day.

You face a cluster fuck of information coming at warp speed under the law of Crofton. You were made or broken during driver training. If you cocked up, they would know, they would always remember your name and not forget your face. Even if you didn't always agree with what an instructor said, you just nodded and smiled.

The daily routine always starts the same, up early to prep the car; every inch must be spotless and clean. Tyres, brakes, fluids checked, then an hour's debriefing on the previous day. Learning from your mistakes is an important part of the training, and they make sure you understand anything you did wrong.

Next, it's a 30–40-minute simple drive, but to me it was like I was back doing my first driving test. I felt nervous and sweaty. I didn't want to get anything wrong. It was pure pressure, and you knew it could change your life. Added to the tension is the knowledge that you have two officers, alpha males, laughing at your every move. You realise that this is just basic driver training, and you have so much more to learn.

Week after week it's the same, learn, drive, debrief and repeat. Their notebooks out, they would tell you to drive from Crofton to Bridlington, using the A614 and A19. What the fuck? Where am I? I've forgotten which way is Bradford, or how I get onto the M62. My instructor is like the silent menace, writing, constantly assessing. You wanted to grab the pen and scream, 'I'm doing nothing wrong, what the hell are you writing.'

'There's been a stabbing in Hull, officer down. Go, go, go,' your instructor shouts. 'Shit, what's going on,' I'm now confused, I'm panicking. My mind is trying to work. I don't know where I am to start with and now, I must react like a professional driver. I need to get to the scene as soon as I can. I just wish I knew where the scene was. I'm trying to read signs at 70mph in a 30mph speed limit. I'm hearing instructions, 'watch your braking,' 'where's your smooth gear change?' I'm questioned as to why I didn't turn right when I should have done so. 'What is the speed limit?' 'What did the red sign say?' It goes on for five hours every day, I am absolutely knackered. It lasts three weeks and it's relentless, but what a great learning curve.

Then it's finally here, the driving test from Hell. You wait, your stomach is churning and finally, it's your turn. They shout your name out. 'PC 1965 Pearson to the car, please.' It reminds me of a 'Police Academy' film, but it's not 'Tackleberry,' It's me, and it's very real. I look at the clock, it's 8.45 am. I've been on and off the loo since the early hours having panic poos. I couldn't eat any breakfast and now I'm shaking like a shitting dog. It means so much to me to pass. I need to pass; please let me pass.

A normal driving test is a doddle compared with the police test. It starts with smooth driving, location awareness, basic commands and open speech. Then, before you know it, you are doing 'blue light' runs with activated light and sirens, speeding through red lights, and driving on the wrong side of the road into oncoming traffic. It's left to you to decide; are you driving to a police standard or is it too dangerous? If it's the latter, you are back to division without your permit. If you pass, you are jubilant, it's like winning the lottery, only it's the 'loner Astra' you have won back at division.

So, you've done it, you have your basic police driving permit. Next stop, become a traffic cop. The wait can be so damn long. You are hoping a vacancy comes up to apply for the job. You do not know how many are going for the role you want. It can be 600 applications for 20 jobs. You just pray you get through the paper sift and pass the internal interview. Even then, it's not over, you must wait for a posting and that can take years.

Once in, you start at the bottom by becoming a traffic aide for two years, but not before you have gone through an advanced traffic law course and done your advanced driving course. This is not dissimilar to the standard course, but more intense, faster and harder. Four weeks of non-stop high-speed driving with no allowance for a mistake. No dangerous actions are permitted; like on 'Top Gun' when they go to Miramar. You are driving the best you can drive, but you know that if you fail the test, you will be back to division and off traffic. If you're very lucky, the driving instructor and traffic inspector may decide it was just a minor issue and you may, I stress, may, get another chance. Now that's what I call real fucking pressure.

I've always admired F1 drivers, they are brilliant at driving and very talented, but they also have crews and millions of pounds thrown at them. Their steering wheels read every inch of the road for them. 20 or 30 crew members are constantly watching. They are told if their tyre has lost 2psi, and to come into the pits. Above all, we do not require them to drive from Bradford to Hull at speed without causing injury to anyone. If they had to, they would be just like us, shit scared initially.

A testing time for me was when, on the advanced course, we drove towards Lincolnshire; fast 'balls out' roads, awesome from a motorcyclist's point of view, but no room for error at all. Once mastered, we moved onto a 'three litre Vauxhall Vectra' or a 'five series BMW'; two plain cars were started together and told you are playing 'cat and mouse.' The message was simple.

'First car does not let the rear car get past. Do nothing illegal, and if the other driver is better than you, let him pass. Do not put any people at risk, show them your talent.'

'Boom,' we are off; driving down empty roads at speeds of 100 to 110 mph; attempting to pass the car in front, on the wrong side of bends, but with an unobstructed view. It is mentally and physically exhausting and unbelievable, the electricity going through you is unreal. It's in the air and we can all feel it; fully grown adults playing big games with big toys.

Bob was my examiner on the ultimate test, known throughout West Yorkshire as a top bloke who pushed you to the limits. He didn't stand for idiots or half-baked drivers. I felt I was doing well, though he referred to me as a 'crazy Keighley bastard' every time I responded. We got three quarters through the test when he told me to drive over to a restaurant. I almost shit myself. I'd blown it, I was going back to division. We stopped and Bob looked at me.

'Well done, Ben, you've done it. Welcome to the Club.'

I was over the moon. I had joined a very elite club and I knew it. I stepped up and shook his hand. I then cried like a six-year-old boy who was refused chocolate on his birthday. All I could say was, 'thank you, thank you,' repeatedly. Bob must have thought I was a right dick. I wasn't remotely mentally ill but must have looked it. We walked into the restaurant, packed with successful candidates. My eyes were puffy, nose running from crying. Like a flash, I asked if anyone had hay fever tablets. I really thought I'd invented a plausible explanation but noticed a few of the firearms boys give me a funny look. I wasn't a crier then but know it's fine to do that now.

I'll never forget those days and, Bob, if you are reading this, thank you for all the time you spent teaching me. I'm honoured and now proud to be called a crazy Keighley bastard.

The training centre at Crofton has now disappeared, replaced by a housing estate. All driver training is now done at Carr Gate in Wakefield. It's still enjoyable but will never have the atmosphere that Crofton had.

As I gained so much experience, the cars I drove became better, the jobs, harder. I had a favourite traffic car; I called her Christine from the horror film. It was a November day, and I was headed towards Toller Lane; I wanted to make a dent in the everlasting offenders who just weren't bothered about the law. It wasn't long before I had issued two mobile phones tickets and one for an unfastened seat belt. I can recall banging on at this driver about the dangers of not wearing a belt. It was then that the radio bleeped, 'Hotel Tango 23, we have a report of a serious head on collision, can you attend?' It was very near, 300 metres as the crow flies.

With the 'blues' flashing, I raced to the scene. Toller Lane has a straight bit of road, then climbs uphill before descending towards Haworth Road Crossroads. As I drove over the peak, I could see carnage ahead of me. A small Suzuki car was embedded in a wall; a male body hung out of the passenger window. A dark coloured Vauxhall Vectra lay upside down in the centre of the road. As I looked around, I heard screams of 'Help me, Help me.' Trying to comprehend what had taken place at the scene, I requested back up. I needed the team's support immediately.

I administered first aid where I could. The man hanging from the passenger side of the Suzuki was elderly. He was unresponsive and had clearly died from his injuries. I checked his pulse and there was no heartbeat. I could see someone trapped in the driver's side, also unresponsive, but he appeared to be breathing. In the back was a woman, around 30, not wearing a seat belt. She had been thrown forward, hitting her head on the dashboard. Her head had split like a nut, from front to back with the force. Cracked fully open, it revealed her skull and brain. The woman was so out of it she kept trying to put her fingers inside her head.

Reassuring her that the ambulance was on its way, I got her to hold her hand on the wound to apply pressure.

In the upside-down Vectra, I found two passengers, one conscious, one not. The conscious male was screaming, his back was clearly broken, he couldn't feel his legs or move. Again, I radioed for urgent backup. The reply came back. 'Do your fucking job and save them.' A bit annoyed, I turned to see the approach to Toller Lane blocked by 'rubber-neckers' and bystanders. They were shouting abuse at me. I told them to get back and stay back, only to receive more abuse and threats.

I was relieved when I heard sirens approaching. Help was finally coming. I saw an ambulance fast response vehicle, trapped by cars abandoned by the 'rubber- neckers,' 80 metres from the scene. I again yelled for them to move back to allow the emergency services through. They ignored me. Two fire engines were also caught up in the traffic jam.

From nowhere came 15 to 20 angry and upset people from the opposite direction. They pulled the adolescent male from the Vectra, paying no regard to his injuries. It turned out they were relations of the people in the Suzuki, throwing a party three doors away from the collision scene. They had heard the impact and seeing the people they loved trapped, injured or dead, the shit hit the fan. I pressed the panic button twice. 'All units, all units, HT23 is code 0 at Toller Lane. All units to respond.' Seconds later, the scene was like a cluster fuck operation.

An officer, paramedic, and firefighters were trying to get things under control. Both sides of the road were now blocked; the emergency services were finding it hard to get through. I saw a paramedic in a headlock, being thrown to the ground and punched, but I was helpless to assist. I was still trying to stop the mob beating the Vectra man to death. People were fighting, there was blood everywhere. God, I felt alone.

Within minutes the area was flooded with uniformed officers who cleared the bystanders and locked the zone down so the investigation could begin. Shortly afterwards we discovered that the family of the dead male had been travelling with two children in the vehicle, who had been thrown into the road as the collision took place. A passer-by had rushed them to hospital before I arrived. They sentenced the driver of the Vectra to four years for the death of the grandfather and injuries caused to the other occupants. It came out in court that hardly any passengers of both cars were wearing seatbelts. Had they done so, the outcome could have been very different. To this day, I cannot stand to see people not wearing seatbelts, and child seats not fitted correctly.

Another of my passions has always been riding motorcycles. If I'm honest though, joining the advanced police cycle unit was an awful choice. Don't get me wrong. It was fun. I got to play the bloke from 'Street Hawk,' or Frank and John from 'ChiPs'. Chris was my tutor and taught me excellent skills. We had so much fun during the course. Chris showed me how to do things on a motorbike that I never thought possible. I think of him now as a great man, fun to be around, who lifted your spirit with his smile.

Four weeks I spent with him, riding to the coast. We enjoyed the sunshine, and I learned to be at the top of my game. It was a good time, but it was also the time that I lost my mum and found out my dad had cancer. I passed the course, but my mum and dad's death and illness overshadowed it. Eight hours a day riding a BMW R1200 RT across England is something any motorcyclist would pay dearly for, but knowing you have lost one parent and the other is dying isn't something that gives cause for celebration.

Weeks later, I was back at division and recommended for my 'Escort and 'Vipex course.' If I passed, I would be escorting oversized vehicles, or doing VIP motorcycle protection, escorting the royal family and heads of state. It was during that course that I visited my dad in hospital and was trying to come to terms with his illness. The tutors understood and were very helpful. Cookie, the chief instructor, told me I could drop out of the course and join the following one. I wanted to continue and felt it was better to take my mind off what was happening in my personal life.

I returned to normal duty, but my dad's health declined quickly. It coincided with a change in duties; I was to escort the Prime Minister, Teresa May. The amount of fear and pressure that put me under is hard to describe. I knew I could do the job, but being told you are protecting the Prime Minister, when you know your head isn't in the game, was a life changer for me. If I fucked up or got it wrong, I felt I would have been hated forever by the boys on the team.

I did the duty, but I knew something wasn't right. Every time I straddled the bike, a motorcycle I knew I could ride well, I was overcome with fear. I didn't know if it was that I feared failing in the job or was becoming aware of my mortality. I saw that riding a motorbike at such high speeds, it was only a matter of time before I binned it, killed myself or someone else. Riding a bike, I knew, was very easy for me, putting on a uniform or riding fast, the same. Put them all together and I crumbled. I felt pure fear, and it burned the inside of me. It was like I knew I was going to die. My bones would be crushed, and I could almost taste blood in my mouth. I was seeing myself in the third person. I was going to watch myself die in pain and alone.

I may have passed each course with success, but Cookie wasn't stupid. I couldn't pull the wool over his eyes. He was a no-nonsense ball buster and wanted perfection. Escorting members of state will either make or break you. If you are not fully there, you are relegated from the team. My dad had now passed, and it filled me with overwhelming emotion.

Going over the speed limit triggered fear for me rather than a smile. I constantly prayed that I wouldn't die. But every day, I felt, was my last.

I spoke to an officer named Adi and told him how I was feeling; I was about to give it up but talking to him made me give it another shot. I had messed everything up the day before, and I had no idea where my mind was taking me. At one point I thought I would have a heart attack after my chest felt so tight. The following day we were to go to Wakefield to escort another VIP. I knew I had to give it my all.

What happened, I really cannot say. I know I was receiving verbal commands, but I wasn't taking them in. I looked in my mirrors to see the VIP convoy going in the opposite direction to me. It confused me; I was meant to be up at the front of the convoy, yet here I was at the back and facing in the wrong direction. I shouted back on the comms. Cookie came back to me and told me to take my time. He had to have realised it was over for me. Looking back now, I realise I was distracted because I was ill, but at the time I didn't have a clue.

All I had worked for was slipping away from me; my childhood dreams were fading fast. I was trying to hold on tight but knew I was losing my grip. I wasn't gaining on the convoy; I just couldn't catch up. I overshot another junction and Cookie radioed me. The sound of disappointment in his voice broke me. He knew I'd lost the plot. I skidded the bike to a halt, nearly dropping it to the ground. I throttled it hard, but the voice in my head told me I had failed. I cried and screamed into my helmet; I was shaking and had tunnel vision. I contacted Cookie and told him, 'I'm done.' He knew what I meant and replied so calmly, 'Back to base.'

My ride back to headquarters was tortuous. I parked up my bike; I was now calmer. Cookie and another officer took me aside. They explained they knew something in me had disappeared and wouldn't ever be coming back. A spark had gone out, my natural instinct was dead. I didn't argue or fight; I knew the same. I was getting to my lowest depths but didn't know why. I was scared for my future. We shook hands. I left heartbroken with my head down, feeling a failure.

It was the last time I rode a police motorcycle, and four months before I finally broke down at work. At home, in my office, I kept my certificates; the awards I worked so hard to earn and was so proud of: 'Standard police driving,' 'Advanced TPAC,' 'Advanced 4 x 4,' 'Escort, Advanced, Motorcycle and VIP Escort'.

I realise now, there are sometimes in your life when you must step back. No one can take away my achievements from me, and it's okay to admit failing. How would I ever know what it feels like to win if I don't know what it is like to fail? My body and mind were trying to talk to me, but my head wasn't open for discussion.

Chapter 5 - My Life on the Line

To say you put your life on the line as a bobby is an understatement. Not only do you put yourself in danger every single day, but it also becomes normal and that can't be normal. Can it?

In 2004, life was good for me. I was young, energetic and full of go. I loved serving the public and tutoring more inexperienced officers. I was in my element. I didn't live with worry; I woke up each day feeling strong in a job I never envisaged leaving. This was my career until the day I retired.

I was still earning my stripes on the beat and getting some wool on my back. The team was great; we had brilliant nights out on the beer, laughing and putting the world to rights. When I say an excellent team, I include my sergeants and inspectors; I had some great ones. These were cops who cared; cops who showed me the right way to do things before you learned to bend the rules. I was in a place where trust and experience went hand in hand. The more I learned, the more my superiors loosened the leash.

If I fucked up, and I did, they took it as a learning curve and gave me some slack. There was one Inspector I had who stood out above the rest. He was a shining light to me. He was well respected in the force and never a nasty word was said against him by anyone. Yes, if you are reading this, Owen, it's you I am talking about. When Owen West said jump, you jumped; but he was fair. If you requested a holiday, he gave you it knowing you had worked hard. He had your back; he protected you, but you knew he was your boss. He got respect. If the shit hit the fan, he was your friend and was there to back you up. Enjoy your well-earned retirement pal.

He was a Chief Superintendent when he left the force, and we are still in contact to this day. He once told me he recalled the time when he went to see my sergeants to discuss my leave application. It wasn't a big issue. I was a top performer, locking up every man and his dog, and our team was flying. I was getting 25 arrests a month alone, not counting the rest of the team, making our supervisors stand out, but Owen told me I couldn't take my leave at Christmas because of the fear that the figures would drop if I was absent.

Apparently, the team got a good talking to, and told to pull their socks up so the supervisors could give me my leave. Thank you, Owen, I never knew that. Also, apologies Owen, you weren't in the first book, but you are in this one.

Two examples of what a great boss can be are the two jobs I'm going to describe now. The first was on a late Friday fight night in Keighley. Adam and I were asked to attend a fight outside a nightclub. The 'K2,' they called it; a very popular place to be on a Friday evening. There were around 30 or 40 people milling about, pushing and shoving, all commonplace, so we had our guards down.

That was our mistake; minutes later I was grappling with a man mountain. A rugby player got abusive and wanted to wrestle. His younger brother was also there having a go, kicking me in the head whilst I locked his big brother up. I could hear my radio bleeping. 'Code O,' shouted the controller, 'officer down.' Within minutes, the street filled with uniformed officers, batons drawn. Leading the group, minus his stab vest, was Owen, baton raised high, screaming 'charge.' He was like an unleashed caged tiger, bodies were thrown left, right and centre as he fought to reach me. The incident was quickly under control; prisoners taken, locked up and charged.

I returned to the nick. Owen took me into his office, looked at me and said, 'absolutely brilliant.' The look on his face said everything as he walked away. He wasn't a man you would want to cross, but he had been there for me as he was for every officer.

Some weeks later I was driving along Keighley Bypass, not paying attention to what was going on; the constant bleeping of the radio drowning my thoughts. I wasn't concentrating. Then Owen's voice came through. 'Get me a unit now.' As fast as I could, I was on the radio asking how I could help him. 'Come lock up this murderer.' What? Had I heard it correctly. I felt myself go cold; a lump rose in my throat. It was like someone had drained all the warm blood from my body.

At some speed, I 'blue lighted' my small Vauxhall Astra to Shipley; skidded to a halt at the location to see several units already present. They had cordoned the scene off. This was serious, and I knew it. I'd also cooked the brakes on the car. The discs were glowing red, smoke bellowing out of the wheels.

I raced to the door of the flat where I was to meet Owen. Strangely, my surprise at the way his voice sounded on the radio was running through my head. This shit was real, and I was here ready to do all I could. Owen then said, 'dead body in there,' pointing to one flat. 'The murderer's in there' he said pointing to another. 'Now go get him.' 'Bollocks,' I thought, 'Is this really happening?' Opening the door, I detected a funny odour; a bit like in a doctor's office, clinical but mixed with the smell of a dirty man's sweat. I could hear really shitty music playing and wanted to shout for them to turn it down. I was busy locking up a top offender here; I needed silence.

At the centre of the room sat a scantily clothed man; his hair cropped short like a home DIY job. I could also see traces of blood around; thinly spread and in need of a good scrub with Ajax and a wire brush. I instructed the man to stand. He obeyed and walked towards me. His eyes were dark, lacking in compassion and love; blank, cold, with something missing. He had no soul in his gaze. It was creepy, and I felt unclean even being near him. I had every right; he had just stamped a man to death in another room. So badly disfigured was the corpse, the victim couldn't be identified. I was face to face with a stone-blooded killer and feeling uneasy.

Grasping his forearm, I quickly cuffed him; cautioned him, and told him he was under arrest for murder. I tried to look him straight in the eyes, keep my calm and my gaze fixed on him. It was hard; my eyes were watering. I couldn't stop myself from blinking. I was glad when I got him strapped into my car. My colleague sat next to him for our safety. Driving to the station, I couldn't stop myself from having images of the horrific crime he had committed. The sheer violence of the offence was just unthinkable.

I could see him through my rear-view mirror just sitting staring at me, only this time I stared back, no blinking, just concentration. If this maniac wanted a staring competition, he was going to get one. I wasn't about to let a man consumed with pure evil beat me. 'I'll find you,' he said. His voice was calm and directed at me. My mind went blank. How do you respond to such a fucking statement? There were no words of wisdom, no one-liner responses. I just replied. 'Yeah, right. In 30 years, when I've retired to Spain, you'll come and get me.' The car fell silent; six miles before we reached the police station. Six miles with a murderous bastard; it was a painful journey. A cat-and-mouse staring game in silence. Not something I thought I would be doing when I put my socks on that morning.

I still had to go through the custody process, and I had to get it right. This was a big case. I needed to get the circumstances correct; ensure that I set my grounds and powers to arrest in concrete. I knew it was all on camera and I had that as backup, but I also know that all eyes were on me. 'Next,' shouts the custody sergeant as I sat waiting in the holding bay. I grabbed my prisoner and walked him to the desk.

I paused for a second and then grinned. My mind had gone, I couldn't say a thing. There I was, holding a murderer and staring at the duty sergeant. Echoing through my mind was the start of the 'Rainbow' theme tune. The sergeant looked at me puzzled, and all that was going through my head was, 'up above the trees and houses, rainbows climbing high,' with a 6ft bear and pink hippo running around.

I then blurted out, 'sergeant, I've attended a flat in Shipley, there's a man who is dead and this is the person who killed him.' 'Officer, I need a little more than that,' came the reply. 'I know, but that's all I've got at this moment.'
It was clear to the sergeant; I was struggling. It's not something you get every day, and she knew it. I had three years in the job, but I was still young and really needed a seasoned officer by my side. As they took him into custody, I knew my learning curve had just gone into orbit.

Thinking back, I realise the entire event overwhelmed me, but Owen gave me the opportunity to learn. He trusted me to deal with the prisoner correctly. I thank him for that. He believed in me then and still does. He was the epitome of what a leader should be and a significant loss to the service. You don't get supervisors like him anymore. They had your total respect, and you would follow them into the abyss. They led from the front. That has all changed now; such men are very rare.

When did I first realise how much my life was on the line? I think it goes back to a Saturday afternoon. It was one o'clock and I was putting on my Altberg boots, lacing them tight before pulling my combat pants over them. I saw two little feet come into view. They belonged to my small son. Faithful bear in hand, he stood by my side, looked into my eyes and remarked, 'Are you coming back daddy?' Time stood still for me. A three-year-old little boy's face full of concern, sweet and innocent, looked up at me. I gazed deeper into his eyes; I had lost count of the times I had come near to death, smelt it, looked it in the face. I had seen, lived and gone through things my son would never know. I never want him to face the pain I have faced as a police officer.

Cuddling him tight to me, I could feel his little heart beating strongly against my chest; his small hand tapping my back. It was then I saw it; if I continued this way, down this path, I would either die or kill somebody. The thought that I could be responsible for a death was something I knew I wouldn't be able to deal with. My conscience would always be clouded. Nor could I bear to leave my kids without their father. My dad had left me to live in Spain, and to this day I feel the pain of that loneliness. The thoughts were tearing me apart.

If you can't see where I am coming from, take yourself into your job and imagine someone walking up to you and smashing you around the head for no reason. It's just they don't like the job you do. What would happen if you were a telephone engineer and went to a house to check someone's line and they stabbed you in the neck? The papers report it as just a part of your job. Would you accept that? So why should police officers accept it?

Only when you are a member of one of the front-line services, do you leave for work wondering if you will come back. On Boxing Day 2003, Ian Broadhurst left for work and never returned. It was the same with Sharon Beshenivsky. Look at the fire service, ambulance service, or Saturday night in A & E. The very people who devote their lives to helping others are the ones facing regular assaults. It leaves a nasty taste in your mouth and consequences for families. When a family member watches as a police officer goes to work, the last thing they want to see is two of their loved one's colleagues standing on the door later that same day.

'Come and work for the police. Be hated by the community. Risk being injured every day. You could even die. Your hours will be long and stressful. You will see things that haunt you for the rest of your days. If you are lucky, your pay will only be frozen for a few years. Fuck up and we'll have you in court faster than we can read you your rights. Join us now! It's a wonderful career.' How many of you would rush to join up if you knew the actual job description?

As a servant of the public, I went out to work every day for 19 years. I was paid by the public, employed by them to protect them. I did so with everything I had in me. In my car kit bag, I carried 40 feet of rope just in case I had to jump into a fast-flowing river to get someone out. Therein lies my first concern. Do I take off my heavy boots and kit first or go straight in? What if it's a small child drowning before my eyes? He comes to the surface; he's gasping for air but goes under again? What would you do? I know I would remove as much of my gear as I could and go straight in. It's my job.

Consider another scenario. They call you to an infants' school. There is a man armed with a knife, stabbing anyone in sight. Children are screaming and bloodied, staff trying to protect them, running in all directions to get out of his way. You're the one who must run towards him, hoping you don't get stabbed. I wonder how many would really put their lives on the line in that way.

Why would I ask or think these things? Why question who I would save, and who I would think twice about? Early in my career, I never thought about such things, but now I have children of my own. If I get seriously injured or die, I leave them without their dad. I do question whether the person in front of me is worthy of risking my own life for. Would I give my life for a person who has just found a cure for cancer? What about an addict or local drunk, you know, who hurts animals? It's your job and you must do what you think is right.

No officer wants to put their life on the line, die on duty or be seriously hurt. No one wants to leave their family devastated and without a parent. Seeing my son at the bottom of those stairs made me realise I didn't want to choose any more. Frequently, death has walked past me, I have felt it breathing down my neck, whispering in my ear, telling me it won't be long; my time's running out.

Over and over my police radio has bleeped to say there is an officer down, urgent assistance needed or 'Code O, I'm hurt.' I've watched officers' line a street in their best dress uniforms as they say goodbye to a fallen colleague; attended a police officer's funeral, listened to their heartbroken family talking about how he loved the job. I don't want to be the person they are speaking about. I want to be the 99-year-old, surrounded by lots of women. Sorry, Milly.

As an officer, you need to come across as strong, unfazed and in control; when you are just a person, the same as the next. You haven't served an apprenticeship to become a superhero. You're not 'Wolverine.' You can't bend metal or see-through walls with your X-ray eyes. You're a man in a stab vest, in a uniform with some spray and a stick. That's it.

I panic, I get scared, I cry, I learn from my mistakes, and I try to cope. I'm human; just like you. When I say I'm scared, I don't mean the 'am I in trouble' scared, or 'is he going to pull a knife on me scared?' That's my job. I mean the 'shit your pants' scared. It's like the time you watched a horror movie and the rookie cop walked down a dark alleyway and you are screaming at him. 'NO,NO,NO,' he's waiting for you.' You then watch as he gets slaughtered by a masked madman with a huge machete.

How many times have I said to myself? 'Don't go in, Ben;' then gone in. I know I'm mad. Every inch of me is saying 'NOOOOOO.' My legs are shaking, I'm weak at the knees. I feel I'm ready to piss myself. I push myself forward only to return to my car and think, 'What the fuck did I do that for?'

There was the time I was single-crewed and had been called to deal with a suspicious male. He was seen entering a warehouse in Denholme; a huge warehouse, I add. It was the size of two football pitches with several floors. So, there I was, just me, with no backup. It was 4am and I was in the middle of nowhere. It was pitch-black, and the wind was howling for all its worth.

I walked around the building checking doors and windows for a sign of any break-in. I was thinking, 'it's a pleasant night to have my head cut off or be skinned alive.' I knew there was someone lurking, that's why I was called, but where was the thieving shit? Preparing to jump me, hurt me badly? Did he want blood, could he see me now? Was I being watched? All these thoughts were running wildly through my head. I then plucked up my courage, took control, and set myself to fuck up anyone who was going to try to damage me.

I was just about at the end of my search when I reached a rear security door. My small torch reflected off the light coming from my police radio. I reached to check the door and it flew open. Shit, all I could see was blackness leading deep into the warehouse. My heart sank, my legs were glued to the floor. I was in a real-life nightmare about to be killed horribly by Michael Myers or Freddy Krueger. The authorities would only recognise me through my dental records.

'X-ray Delta, I'm code six at Denholme,' I transmit and get a positive response; I'm saved. A Bradford police dog unit has heard my calls. I'm relieved to see my friend Simon and his land shark arrive to assist me. You always feel a million times better when there is a dog with you.

We searched the building, top to tail. I knew the dog would sense anyone hiding in the shadows. It would at least give me time to run out with my tail between my legs. There were rooms all over, mess everywhere. It was cold, damp and dusty. We reached the main storeroom with its nine-foot-high ceiling. It was about 40 feet wide with shadows in every corner. Suddenly the fur on the dog's back went up. He had smelt something and was on high alert. Dragging Simon across the room, it stopped at a small doorway.

'Officer with dog,' Simon shouted a warning. My heart sank. We were moments away from grappling with someone. My adrenaline was pumping, and it felt like my heart would burst out of my chest. A bang came from above us; dust fell through the cracks in the boards over our heads. There was someone up there. We could hear them walking calmly and slowly towards the opposite side of the building. Clip clop, the sound of his shoes echoed in the darkness. Even the dog looked scared. Did we go up or? Run to our cars? What would you do?

As a proud West Yorkshire Police Officer, we knew what to do. Fuck it, we are going up. The dog was now thirsty for action and wanted blood. At the door of the room, we knew the intruder was in, we stopped. Simon then kicked it open, let the dog off its lead and bang, the land shark is running into the darkness and out of sight. We could hear it barking and knew it had someone cornered. Fumbling around, we found and flipped the light switch, illuminating the room. There was no one there. It was completely empty: no equipment, no boxes and no burglar or mass murderers. We looked at each, puzzled; the dog was sitting looking at a small window seven feet up. The window was closed but could be opened if someone could reach it whilst stood on something.

The hairs on the back of my neck really stood up as Simon, a shocked look on his face, pointed out two freshly made hand marks in the centre of the window. Without a ladder, it was impossible for anyone to reach the window, plus there was a 40 foot drop at the other side onto hard tarmac. I was officially scared. I had never been that petrified before.

I was desperately trying to compute what was happening, but it wouldn't go in. Where was the man? He had to be hiding, but where? There were two of us, we both saw the dust, heard the steps. I was freaking out; I can't say any other, but I know what I heard and saw. Extremely confused, we left the building. I shoved my hands in my pockets so Simon wouldn't see how much I was shaking. I was scared and couldn't drive off until I'd checked the boot and back seat. I had to be assured no one was hiding there. Back at the station, I had to write my report. How do you do that and make it sound like you're not insane?

Was that my first encounter with the unknown? It wasn't. Let me take you to Toller Lane Police Station. Ask any seasoned officers around Bradford to tell you its stories. The station stands on an old mill footprint. Many say that men died in the old mill before they erected the station. They are said to haunt it now. I'm calling it 'Bullshit with a sprinkle of rubbish on top.'

My view was solid scepticism until one day I came to work around midday. Several spiritual mediums were being led around the station by some traffic cops. They were sensing the building for negative energy and trying to bring peace to troubled souls, I was told. I just wanted to laugh. I had been told stories by several officers but didn't believe any of them. There was this one officer who I knew didn't lie or stand for any shit. When he told me, he thought he had seen something, I listened. Small alarm bells rang. Were they kidding, winding me up, or serious?

Still disbelieving, I dismissed all the stories which were now coming in at least once a week. So, returning to the Denholme story, I returned to the station; I was cold and couldn't get warm, even though the heating in the car was full on. I needed a break, a hot brew and some chocolate to spark me back up. Walking around the warehouse had sapped me of my energy. Still filled with fear, I pulled into the Toller Lane car park. It was vacant; the rest of the team were still out.

The station lights were on sensors, so the whole place was in darkness as I arrived. You needed to walk beneath the sensors to turn the lights on. If this didn't happen, they automatically turned off to save power. I opened the rear door into the stairwell and the light came on. I went into the traffic office, again the light flipped on. I was warming up now. I felt relaxed and safe in my second home. I was hidden away behind a huge metal gate, only accessed by security card. I could now fill my belly and begin to chill out.

I needed to eat to get the energy to do my report. I would be in bed in four hours' time, but I had to do my paperwork first. Sat at my desk, I typed, occasionally looking up to re-focus my eyes. It was then that I spotted a faraway hall light illuminate, then another, this time closer to me, and another. Someone else had finished their duty and was coming up the corridor or leaving from another office. I continued my report but found it harder and harder to concentrate. I almost shut my eyes; I was so tired.

I knew I would sleep well when I got to bed. Taking my glasses off and rubbing my eyes, I opened them to see a dark figure walk across the doorway to the traffic office. It walked left to right, activating lights as it did so. Then it disappeared out of sight. As I typed, it re-appeared, walking again from right to left. I had almost completed my report when the figure appeared just above the level of my computer. I could now see it was a male. 'Kettle's boiled if you want a brew.' I shouted but got no reply. I clicked print, got up, and walked to the printer to collect my completed statement. I repeated my question, again no answer.

'I know it's early morning, we are all tired but there's no need to be rude,' I shout.

I still got no answer, so walked to the corridor, a bit miffed. It's 30 feet long and I was shocked to see it totally empty. I felt uneasy now, so returned to the office. I was relieved to see one of my teammates had just returned. I told him about the earlier job at the warehouse and what had just happened. I added, 'I think I must be going mad because of tiredness.' He agreed and took the piss out of me. I sat back to do some more typing and saw the shadowy figure again but this time my teammate shouted, 'don't freak but I've just seen it.' We both panicked, dashed to the door and scanned the corridor, it was still empty. Was it a ghost? I can't say, I have no idea what it was, but we both saw it and neither of us could explain it. Make your own mind up.

It's an example of what I've stated previously. We are just humans in a uniform; someone's brother, sister, daughter, son. The things we feel are the same as you feel. We get just as scared as anyone else. The big difference is that our job conditions us to hide our emotions, show no fear, see only in black and white, and know the law to the nth degree. They teach us to assess, assess and assess some more. There are no grey areas, the evidence is the evidence and must be collated so facts don't lie.

During my younger days, I used to thrive on all of this. I wanted to work every hour I could. My supervisor would ask if anyone wanted to work two week shifts of seven on and three off, twelve-hour sessions. Damn right I would, I'm single, I'll get more money in my pocket and spend days off in bed. Bring it on.

By day three I was on my knees, ruined by five hours sleep; fuelling myself on 'McDonald's' and shitty, warm, expensive petrol station sandwiches. Day six came, and I felt physically ill. My diet and sleeping patterns were poor, and I didn't help myself by eating bowls of cornflakes swilled down by with five cans of 'Carling' every time I got home.

People asked if I ever shut down, logged off or had a rest. 'No, it's part of me. What I signed up for,' was my stock reply. I was proud to tell them, even on my rest days, I could still arrest people and lock them up. It was my job; I was proud of it. We are not in America, and I don't have to stop at a border. If I see a dangerous driver or a 'fail to stop,' it's like 'Cannon Ball Run.' I'm after it, not stopping until I get to it.

Once I went to Birmingham to collect a prisoner. Up ahead, I could see a car driving from side to side. It was about 500 meters in front, but I could see its taillights clearly. Outside my area, I was unsure of the roads. I just knew I was at a junction on the M62, west bound approaching the M60. Then I spotted another car, a BMW X5 doing the same. I wasn't sure what force we were in or the radio channel I should be on. I spoke to my oppo; we decided we needed to have a cheeky look.

As I gained on both vehicles, I realised the X5 was a Greater Manchester Police motorway unit, and the vehicle in front was refusing to stop. 'PASS,' illuminated the X5 on its rear matrix board. 'Shit,' they thought I was here to help. I knew he was on his radio yelling for me to get past and assist. He'd be thinking. 'What's this 'knobber' behind doing? Having a good look? Chatting about what he's been watching on TV?' Panicking now, I radioed West Yorkshire's control. 'HT23', I shouted. 'We're in a pursuit on the M62, west bound.'

The radio went mental. Every traffic vehicle in West Yorkshire was shouting, wanting to join the fun. Our control room now thought the pursuit was in West Yorkshire, not realising it's the GMP X5 in pursuit. I tried to explain we were near Manchester, behind a vehicle and a police car. They were engaged in the pursuit. 'Go to the local channel,' my control room instructs me. That was easier said than done. Our vehicle lists every force's channel from Northumbria to Sussex. Each main channel has 15 to 20 other operational local channels. There was my fat-fingered oppo banging every channel button on the keypad in a frenzy.

Blue lights and sirens were wailing as another police car passed us. Both the driver and front seat passenger were giving us disgusted looks and shaking their heads. They couldn't understand why we were there and why weren't helping them. 'Get the bloody channel,' I screamed at my oppo. 'We need to help our boys.' 'X-ray Whiskey West Yorkshire, urgent ....' No reply. He tried another channel, again silence. Then, BOOM, it happened. The biggest humiliation and kick in the balls ever. We were illuminated brightly by a million candle watt bulb, targeted by the local police helicopter trying to identify us.

Two more police vehicles passed, followed by a firearms unit and dog van. All were staring as they went by, totally confused. I grinned at them and mouthed 'sorry, I'm not crap, really I'm not.' 'Hotel Tango urgent go to GMP OPS2,' my control room yelled at us. 'Quick, get it,' I shouted. Big fingers found the channel and we were good to go. 'X-ray Whiskey Hotel Tango 23, West Yorkshire,' I shouted over the air. Silence, then a voice said, 'Aww West York's, so you are coming to join us then?' 'STOP, STOP, STOP,' came next and all vehicles halted. Police were everywhere, wrestling the suspect to the floor like a toy doll. Sheepishly and feeling stupid, I looked at the other officers who were now giving us an enormous round of applause. Still in the helicopter's spotlight, I took a bow, jumped in my car and made off feeling like a right ass. I knew we had let West Yorkshire Police down. We had let our guard down and taken our eye off the ball. That's something you can't do as a traffic cop.

Several times I have stated that we are never off duty. A police officer doesn't go home and switch off, that's impossible. I was once off duty and enjoying a night out with my brother. Our girlfriends and some other friends were with us, having a quiet night out in Shipley at a curry house. We were having a good time until a fight broke out behind us between a father and his son. It was a violent affray with no punches held back. In simple terms, they were knocking the living shit out of each other. Two of the women with us were heavily pregnant, so there was no choice but to act.

We grabbed both males and threw them into the street. I wasn't fucking about with pregnant women around. Fight, if you want to, but not next to me and mine. I had settled back down to my meal when CRASH, the windows on the door of the premises shattered. Father and son had now teamed up and were attacking the restaurant.

The doors pinned shut, we waited for the uniformed police to arrive and arrest them. Ironically, the father then feigned a heart attack in the doorway. Acting skills honed, he flickered his eyes shut, only to become alert again when an officer pulled his earlobes and dragged him across the footpath into a waiting van. Should we have left them to fight? No, my job is to protect the public on or off duty.

So, what happens when you know the criminal personally? On one occasion I had parked my motorbike up and gone into the Co-op in Baildon to buy myself a drink. I saw an old school friend I'd not seen for years. I remembered he used to look after me in middle school and held my brother in high esteem. The lad was always a tough nut, though; not to be messed with. Well, I was walking around, my helmet in my hand, and I saw my pal kneel and fill his old school sports bag with around £100 of the finest steak cuts.

I watched in amazement as the cheeky bastard, brazenly, in front of another shopper, who clearly ignored what was going on, continued his pilfering. Now, I work up to 80 hours a week and still can't afford such luxuries, so I'm fucking sure if I can't have them, he's not going to. I was fucking livid. The staff knew me, saw me and saw him. If I acted, I knew I would have to go to the local nick and do a statement, putting on hold my bike ride in the Lake District with colleagues.

I literally stomped out of the Co-op down another aisle. I knew he had to pass the tills and leave the store before I could arrest him for committing an offence. As I got to the door, I heard, 'Officer, shoplifter.' Bollocks, I turned to see this well-built ex-friend running towards me with the best cuts of prime steak under his sweaty armpit. 'STOP THERE,' I shouted at him. Everyone in the shop turned to look at me, confusion on their faces. He stopped running, looked at me and begged. 'Please Ben, let me go, you can have the meat.'

My heart slumped with pity. I knew he had hit hard times, and he had always had my back in school, but a crime was a crime, and I was a copper. A fact he well knew, but it didn't stop him. He had shown no respect for me. If he had, he would have shoplifted at the other side of Bradford, not in my area.

A slight scuffle went on in the doorway, but he decided the outcome would be inevitable and gave himself up. I escorted him into the security office and waited for a unit to arrive. I'd done my bit and now it was over to them. I left with a bitter taste in my mouth. It felt like I'd let my old self down. But, as an old sergeant once told me, if you patrol your own area where you live, your loyalties will be questioned.

My worst off duty incident came later. I had met Rick, my friend, for a drink in the local pub. I had been on a detox and was gagging for a cold pint. We arrived at the 'Shoulder of Mutton,' now demolished, and ordered our drinks. We were prepared for a good old knees-up and chat. The first pint touched my lips like velvet as it slid down my throat.

In the next instance, the door flew open, smashing as it did so. In ran a petite, ginger-haired woman, distraught and screaming, 'He's dead, he's dead.' 'Fuck me,' I thought. I had no idea what was going on, but I knew enough to prepare myself for action. 'Ben!' yells the barman. I stood and went to the frightened, confused woman and recognise her as one of my old Grammar school teachers.

It was impossible to console her, so I ran to the door to check what was happening. A car was in the middle of the road, behind which lay a body. 'Dial 999,' I instructed the barman. I then ran across the wet carriageway to see blood running down the kerb and drain area. A male was laying on his front, face down, his back completely ripped open revealing his bones and organs; his torn flesh lay on the tarmac. Rick came out to see what was going on; I told him to keep the woman secure. 'Don't let her drink anything,' I told him. I then called the incident in, informing the ambulance control room that I was off duty. The injured man had no pulse and was unresponsive.

They dispatched a unit before putting me on to the police control. The call was answered by a friend who could sense the panic in my voice. Strangely, when you have your uniform on, your armour, you go into automatic pilot. In a police car; you could block the road; in a white tee-shirt, best jeans and new white trainers, you feel different; vulnerable and alone.

I told my colleague that it was a 'fatal,' and he dispatched several units to the scene. 'Do what you can, Phil is on his way,' I was instructed. Phil is a good friend, a real man's man. In the office, I used to take the piss out of him. I used to tell him that if I was a woman.... I would then wink at him. He would wink back and reply, 'if I was a woman, I'd most likely let you.' We'd both laugh, enjoying the fun. Phil is now retired.

I tried to stem the bleeding with my hands, but it was just too heavy. I felt useless, but there was little I could do. I looked up to see a 4 x 4 vehicle. A male stood by it, his face pale, his look blank. He was around 50ish. I knew instinctively that this was the driver who had been in the accident. It was clear by the way he was holding himself; it had broken him.

I felt a tap on my shoulder. It was an off-duty firefighter. Pointless as I knew it was, we still tried to perform CPR on the male despite his terrible injuries. We had to; it could have been my dad laying there. A short while later, an off-duty nurse joined us. There couldn't have been more help available if you had planned it. It took me back to a time when an old pal, called Dave, an ex-traffic cop, got knocked off his bike in a remote area. The first person to arrive on the scene had been an off-duty surgeon who had, without doubt, saved his life and even left his own family to take Dave to hospital.

That's what you find with the emergency services, on or off duty, they come to assist. None of us would think twice about getting stuck in. It's what makes us special. They placed the injured man in the ambulance, but the paramedic looked at me and shook his head. I knew the male wouldn't survive. I watched as they 'blue lighted' him to hospital. We had tried but failed. Phil then took over the scene, and I was free to go back and finish my pint. I would give a full statement on the following day when I had my head together.

No one said a word as I walked back into the pub, blood on my knees, my trainers and trickling from my hands. I went straight to the toilets to wash myself. As I did so, a single tear ran down my cheek. I didn't cry, but I needed to. Adrenaline still flowing, I pushed my emotions into my magic box, the one sunk deep within my soul. I returned to my seat at the bar, but the pint no longer felt that enticing. I left the pub and walked home alone. I would have a hot shower and scrub myself clean, trying to think if there was something else, I could have done.

My trainers and jeans thrown in the bin; I went to bed. I wanted to cry, should have cried, but I couldn't. I could feel the water pushing forcefully at the dam wall, but I still refused to allow it to break through. I didn't know then what I know now, of course. Had I known I would have cried buckets all night long. Instead, it remained trapped inside the black box, hidden away for no one to find.

Chapter 6 - Human to Machine

The only thing that there is no training manual for, no advice given to you, is for those moments when your human emotions kick in. You must rely on your own ability to cope with such things and deal with it as you see fit. You must ask yourself at some point; however, when does the machine run out of oil and the human being take over?

Can you understand the warning signs and know how to forgive yourself if human emotion pops out midway through a briefing, or whilst you are taking a statement? Maybe it will happen in the middle of ASDA with seven people staring at you.

143

I remember once I had to sit on Ilkley Moor, alone with a man who had committed suicide. He had taken a shotgun, placed it in his mouth and pulled the trigger. I had to stay with him while mortuary technicians arrived. It was so surreal. I sat by his side talking to him like I was talking to a friend; watching the sheep that surrounded us, casually eating grass. Parts of my new friend's head were missing; that's what a shotgun does to you.

I couldn't do anything to change the desperation that had led to this man committing suicide in such a brutal way. What I could do was to accord him the respect his family would want. They would want to know that the last person alone with their son had cared about him. It was eerie sitting there with a corpse, and I could only hope the mortuary technicians would turn up soon. At that stage, I was forgetting my training as my emotions took control. I could have sworn that I saw the man move. The more I stared, the more I was convinced he turned his head to look at me and then back again quickly. Your imagination plays tricks on you in such circumstances, and all the robotic training in the world can't stop it happening. It took almost three hours before they arrived to collect the body.

Next day I went to the butchers to collect my usual meat parcel and added in a juicy steak as a treat. 'Cut it an inch thick,' I told him. I thought I was okay. Last night's memories and emotions had faded. But as soon as the bandsaw entered the bone of the meat, I burst into tears. The staff and other customers looked at me as if I was mad. I wasn't, I just needed the release, and I couldn't show my emotions in front of my teammates. It was just something you didn't do.

The problem is you don't know when your emotions are going to take over and the human in you is going to rise to the surface. On another occasion I was being tutored by Sam during my ten weeks' training. We attended a sudden death in Bradford Royal Infirmary. It was nothing too unusual. An old lady had passed and needed her jewellery removing. I approached the door to the room she was in and felt myself welling up. I couldn't stop it; tears flowed out of nowhere, but it was the only way I could deal with the weight of what I was seeing and doing. Others turn to alcohol and let it consume them, but I drank little, so my emotional release came out differently.

In later years, as my police career was ending, it had become more complex. I was so burned out by that time. Experiencing fear, real deep fear, was hard. I had seen too much by then to by affected in the same way. If I felt fear, it was because of my inability to do anything about what I had seen. I couldn't change things.

The thought of dying and leaving my family, or my family being hurt, always cast a shadow over my mind, but as a police officer, it's one you must live with. Officers are conditioned to protect you; they may come across as hard-nosed and lacking in emotion, but their care is there. It's deep down, but the mechanical way in which they teach you to do your job, train you to survive, is always at the forefront of your mind.

With the amount of conditioning that takes place, you find it hard to switch off when your shift is over. You are expected to do so, even told to 'leave it at work.' But how hard is that? You forget what normal is. This is where I failed, I couldn't separate my job from my personal life. Many officers are good at doing that. I wasn't.

As a traffic officer, you must be able to jump into your own or any other car and drive to an exceptionally high standard; switch off everything and concentrate solely on what you are doing. You must know traffic law in its entirety; be skilled in pursuit guidelines and know the location of every other police unit you are relying on. Your head is like an A to Z; the roads and layouts imprinted on your brain.

Firearms officers have a different type of conditioning. They must be able to select a weapon and take someone's life if necessary. Hesitation kills and it could be you who ends up dead. No one wants to take someone's life but put yourself in their position. Imagine a lone gunman is walking through the streets where you live, shooting everyone in sight. A firearms officer will attend without a second thought, even though their life may then be at stake.

Once in position, the officer gets the shooter in his sights and pulls the trigger. The threat is removed, and civilian lives saved. For the officer it goes far deeper; in an instance it changes his life. Yes, he did everything required, all that they trained him to do. He carried out his duty as a trained firearms expert, exactly as he was conditioned to do. Then, he had to go home, to his dreams, to his changed perception about the value of life.'

Could I have pulled the trigger? I have massive mental health issues now because of the job. Had I been on that street, the man who had to kill another to save lives, what would I have done? It hurts me to think about it. I've tried to give you examples of when the fear sets in and the conditioning takes a back seat. I want you to understand that police officers are human like anyone else. We are not machines but highly trained professions doing our job.

2010 was another time I will never forget feeling fear. I was on mobile patrol with my tutor and teammate, John. It was a warmer than normal night, the windows of our patrol car were wound down. We patrolled the back streets of Keighley before getting onto the main drag with North Street and Cavendish Street. The evening was lovely, and it was great to be on patrol, chatting and taking in the night's hustle and bustle.

At the time I was a passenger, taking a break from driving. 'Did you hear that?' John asked, looking at me. 'A stabbing on North Street at the Livery Rooms. Did you get that?' I responded immediately. 'Show us as attending,' I told the control room. John's driving was amazing; smooth and fluid, I was pinned to my seat whilst different scenarios went through my head. 'Ambulances code 6,' we heard over the radio. That means they had arrived on scene.

We then heard that the CCTV had picked up the incident and were reporting officers in need of urgent assistance. John switched into automatic driving mode. We didn't speak until seconds later as we skidded around the corner onto North Street. I was shocked at the sight before me. Ambulances were everywhere. Officers and civilians had pinned the suspect down; he was being handcuffed. People were walking around dazed, pure fear and confusion on their faces; dark red blood covering them from head to toe.

John leapt from the car and began co-ordinating the scene. Calmly, he radioed control, giving a blow-by-blow account, at the same time checking who was injured and who wasn't. I grabbed my green first aid box and made my way to the door of the building. All I could hear were screams of confused and fearful people. As I entered the bar, it shook me to my core. There were bodies everywhere; some still conscious, others not. Blood trickled onto the floor and ran into the cracks of the floorboards.

Blood-drenched towels were on those tables, still upright. Other tables were tipped over, glass was all over the place. I counted at least six or seven people who had been stabbed multiple times and were fighting for their lives. My anxiety level was soaring, adrenaline pumping through my veins. People were relying on me to help. I spotted a girl to my right; she was barely conscious but lifted her arm up to attract my attention. I dropped to my knees into a pool of her blood and began checking her wounds.

I was looking for entry points and lifted her top at the back. There was a large hole in the back of her chest towards the right of her should blade. The hole was at least two or three inches long. I couldn't see how deep it went. I tried to dress it with bandages, but they kept disappearing into her wound. She was passing in and out of consciousness. I was thankful when a paramedic I knew stepped in to help. Together we tried to stabilise her. Sheer desperation hung in the air alongside the warm smell of blood. With a look of 'fuck this,' on my colleague's face, we carried her straight out of the pub and into a waiting ambulance. She had minutes to get to hospital before she would have died.

Ambulances blocked the street by this time. Paramedics were finding it difficult to cope with so many injured. Police officers were following ambulances to hospital to 'blue light' medics back to the scene to continue dealing with the wounded. It was so chaotic, a police officer had to drive the ambulance to hospital to free up the paramedics, so they could work on the wounded in the rear.

I ran back into the building to help more people. It really was a disorderly scene. I was covered in blood as I gave first aid to victims. It was an upsetting place to be, but a place where I was needed. These were people who had come out for a few drinks and an enjoyable evening. Now they were fighting for their lives at the hands of a madman with a knife.

As I worked on another victim, I noticed a movement in the bar area. Initially, I paid no attention, but the sound of chuckling made me look up. There, at the bar, stood three young men. It angered me to realise that when the trouble kicked off, they had just stood by and watched, drinking their beer. Now, they seemed to find it funny. I lost it, jumped up and grabbed one of them by the shirt. 'Fuck off out of here now,' I shouted in his face; the blood on my hands marking his pristine shirt with deep red fingerprints. I escorted him from the building, his feet hardly touching the floor. His two friends hurried after him.

It took a good hour or more to get the victims into ICU or casualty. The paramedics and officers alike had done everything possible to administer first aid and lifesaving treatment. There was a strange stillness when John and I stood outside the building. Officers were looking at each other in silence. The atmosphere had gone from zero to a thousand in less than a second. Pure fear consumed my body again, but training and conditioning had allowed me to have given my best.

Back at the station, I changed out of my bloodied clothes. I was trying to rinse the blood, which had now congealed, from my arms and hands. The suspect turned out to be a young lad, no older than 20 years. He was a paranoid schizophrenic. Before going to the 'Livery Room,' he had already stabbed a man, just walking innocently in the street, in the chest. He continued creating mayhem in the pub, stabbing drinkers at random. Brave members of the public had overpowered him and held him until police officers arrived and arrested him.

There is a fine line between life and death. Often someone is just in the wrong place at the wrong time. No amount of training can change the fragility of life: a knife doing? My feelings are mixed with the joy of seeing my kids so happy, a stab, half an inch too far in the wrong direction, a speeding car on a wet road, a moment of distraction by the driver. It's all it takes to become another number, another fatality. I am trained to a high standard, but I became more '1965,' my collar number, than Ben Pearson the human.

Over the years I have watched as the police force has changed. Technology has overtaken everyday policing. As a fresh recruit, I would arrest someone at a 'domestic,' return to work, submit a report, handwritten on paper. That would be sent off somewhere, get collated, and someone would type it into a computer system. There were no such things as mobile phones used for police duties, and we would ask to use the complainant's land line to phone CIS to ring in the crime. They would be given a crime number for their insurance and left at the scene.

We all have mobile phones with internet connections now, so now we record our own crimes cutting out the person in the middle. Computerisation has brought about a more streamlined service, but also more pressure on front line officers. The procedure now is that a call, comes in for a crime. At the scene you talk to the complainant, take a detailed statement on your device. It sounds better than older procedures, but, and a big but, when I trained, there were no computerised systems like today, so I was never taught the ins and outs of them. If I was a 16-year-old with a degree in technology, I would be okay, but I'm not, I'm a 44-year-old who left school believing that Gammon was a fish.

It doesn't stop there. You then check the scene to collect evidence before leaving. If we make an arrest, it's back to the station, they exhibit all evidence including clothing from the accused, a statement from the officer and CCTV content, if available. Only when all that is done can interviewing the suspect begin. That, of course, is after the three hours' wait whilst he's checked out by a nurse after he complains we have beaten him up. Another three hours and his solicitor arrives to spend 40 minutes consulting with him. Finally, the interview occurs, where the burglar smiles 'no comment' all the way through.

It's now passed to the Crown Prosecution Service, requiring hours and hours of paperwork from the arresting officer. You wait tentatively for the CPS to come back, telling you to charge all offences. You are happy, the criminal is off to court Monday morning. All weekend he will receive bed-and-breakfast service. He's acting as a tough guy, and you need to watch him through the two-inch-thick glass on his cell door until he needs a shit and sheepishly asks you to turn your back. Here, the well-oiled machine has gone into action and worked. The offender is going to pay for his crimes.

Come Monday morning, you are back on the scrote's hunting ground. He's free again and carrying his new DVD; the one he has found miraculously in the bushes and is taking to the pawnshop. Bollocks......'What happened at court?' I ask. 'Not enough evidence, boss, so CPS dropped the charges.' 'Sure', I think. 'You were outside of a burgled house at 4am in the morning. It was 16 miles away from your home. You matched the full description of the suspect on CCTV and had the claimant's keys to his Mercedes car.'

He smirks, he's told the judge he was out walking his dog. The dog got off his lead and ran away. He was searching for his dog when he found the keys and was just about to ring the police when he was arrested. Cynical I may be. I know he is lying, why? His mouth is open, and words are coming out.

It's more than annoying when you know there are some criminals with 54 convictions against their name. You see them bailed for robbery and burglary because it isn't about what we know; it's all down to what we can prove. To go before a judge or magistrate, you need to prove your case 100%. The defence will look for anything. I've seen cases thrown from court because we have not passed a form to their defence, or the wrong officer collected a piece of evidence. The reality is that the system is overrun, and prisons are full. The machinery may be in place, but sometimes the legal system lets you down.

Visualise this. It's 2008, I'm out on a night shift with my tutor John. I've mentioned him in 'Handcuffed Emotions,' an awesome guy and a terrific officer. We are on patrol and come across a black BMW minus its number plates. It's outside a house, but still on the main road. We can see the seat belts are clipped in their holders to stop it beeping, and to look as though worn by the driver, if being followed from behind.

So as not to spook anyone, we park higher up the road. Under the cover of darkness, I record the car's chassis number. The information shows us a violent male who has just been released from jail. We see he has links to firearms and other markers saying, 'DO NOT STOP.' There is no tax or insurance, and the driver is thought to be disqualified. We inform control, and the divisional inspector tells us he is putting in a firearm plan as quickly as possible.

The male suspect exits from the house and walks back to his car. Off he speeds, doing a U-turn further up the road. Instantly, we follow the vehicle. We are in robot mode. He is clocking up 60 mph in a 30 mph zone. 'Follow at a safe distance,' we are told; 'Firearms are on their way.' It was clear he had sighted us and was making off. A pursuit was underway but as quickly as it started it ended. He had turned right into a long driveway and fled on foot towards the rear of the house.

With only 10 to 15 feet between us, John and I are on his tail. Next, he runs into the rear of an enclosed garden with 8 ft high walls on either side. There is nowhere for him to go, nowhere to run, but he's vanished. I look down; I see his legs coming from under the bumper of a camper van. I shout for him to stay there and stay down before proceeding to pull him from under the van. It takes seconds only for the shit to hit the fan.

Keep visualising. I'm 6'2" tall and weigh 16 to 17 stone. I work out and I'm in good shape. John, at 5'10", is also very strong. The runner is around 5'4", a little wide and of no significant physique. He growls like a dog as I pull at his legs. He stands up quickly as I get behind him and put him in a 'half nelson' choke hold. Seconds later, I find myself on the floor with this male stamping on my chest. How I got there, I can't tell you. I can only think I got knocked out.

The next thing I remember was seeing John on the man's back, repeatedly smashing him over the head with the police radio and shouting, 'stop resisting.' The male responded by stamping harder and harder on my chest. I heard a crack; something had snapped, and I was scared now, 'shitting my pants,' scared. How injured was I was going to be? He then pulled me up to his face by my stab vest. My nose inches from his, face to face. White froth was coming from each side of his mouth as he growled obscenities at me. He acted like a rabid dog. I was confused, I knew there were lights spinning everywhere but I couldn't think or get up.

I also feared for John, I was younger than him and should have been protecting him. I tried again to get up and succeeded, only to be slammed back to the floor by this 13 stone shit house. In horror I realised it wasn't just me who had been overpowered, but John also, as the hulk picked him up and threw him over me. We are talking about seconds. But it seemed much longer. It was a cluster fuck. Then, in a flash, the assailant was off and running towards a graveyard.

I shouted to John that he was getting away and to go after him. John, himself injured by a bad beating, pressed his 'Code 0' button repeatedly on his radio. Help was on its way in the form of a helicopter and several firearms units. Half of Bradford Division was also en route.

Incensed and in pain, I got to my feet, ran across the road and gave chase through the graveyard. An X99 police helicopter hovered ahead, I could see nothing of the man, but I wasn't ready to give up. I was fucking fuming, a red mist all around me. How hurt I might be I didn't care, I needed to get this man. I skidded to a stop in the undergrowth as the graveyard came to a dead end, a flowing river at its boundary. The X99 couldn't get a thermal image either, so I realised he had to have jumped into the river and swum downstream.

I walked back to the car; the adrenaline was wearing off, and I felt pain. I had taken a real beating. Neither my body nor my pride liked it. Officers checked me over for injuries. They placed the offender on West Yorkshire's most wanted list. Back at the station, John and I just stood and looked at each other. The suspect had served both of our arses on a plate, and we knew it. It was then a CID officer came into the traffic office. So high was the level of the criminal's activity, they urgently wanted statements so they could gather a team together to hunt for the man. My chest was hurting and clicked when I coughed, but it didn't matter. They needed the statement. Battered and bruised, I just started writing. I knew I hadn't written according to correct police method. Instead of 'R vs Turnbull,' etc. I wrote it in the third person.

If I was in that situation now, I would tell the CID officer to wait until I could collect my thoughts and think about the full facts rather than just winging it for speed. My statement, instead of amounting to five or six pages, was a paltry two. It should have been in depth and flowing, but it ended up like a four-year-old's story book.

We were so pleased when the man walked into the police station four days later, his solicitor in tow. John and I were on a high. He would soon be in a prison cell, game over. Well, I thought it was game over. How wrong was I. It wasn't long before the CID officer returned and told us the Detective Sergeant wanted to see us? We were going to be commended for our efforts, I wrongly thought.

The DS's face looked like a slapped arse as we walked in. Other officers were working. 'Sit down,' he commanded. He then tore strips off us. He condemned our statements, accusing us of lying, fabrication, and misinformation. Any ideas of praise flew out of the window.

A blank look on my face, I switched off. I could see the DS's lips moving, but I had zoned out. My thoughts turning to what a twat he was. Words like 'misconduct,' 'illegal' and 'let down,' flowed over me. I felt myself shaking and imagined a bull's eye appearing on the right side of his chin. I wanted to deck the bastard. Other CID officers were all listening, and I got angry and more upset. I had been out on the streets, beaten up, bruised and battered whilst they sat in their cosy office, getting a nice hot brew brought to them. Whilst doing what? Spending six hours ripping our statements to bits, when we only had twenty minutes to write them. Plus, we were in no fit condition to do so.

It transpired that CCTV surrounded the accused's family home to protect them from repercussions, knowing that their relative had fingers in every criminal pie out there. They were paranoid something would come back to haunt them. CID had viewed the recording, and while they saw everything was just as I had written it, there was one point that wasn't accurate. I had clearly stated that I hadn't lost sight of him when he ran. The video showed that I had. We were seen running up the drive a few feet behind the suspect. He then turned left and fell straight to the floor and rolled under the camper van. Two seconds later, I turned left, saw him and pulled him out. That was said to be an outright lie. I was now in danger of going to prison and becoming someone's husband on 'D' wing.

Why was this happening? It was because I had forgotten I was a robot. The pain of my injuries had taken over and brought the human out in me. I flipped and lost it big time. 'How fucking dare you?' I snapped. 'Don't call me a fucking liar. You can't do what I do, you don't have the skill, back bone or ability to do it.' My blood was boiling, and I knew I was stepping over the mark, but there was no going back now. I stood up, kicked the empty chair by my side over and shouted. 'I'm walking away now before I do something I regret.'

John and the DS stood there, blank faces, open-mouthed. I marched from the office, banging the door behind me. It was when I calmed down, I thought, 'what the fuck have I just done?' Months later, we were called to court for the case. There was an almighty legal battle taking place between prosecution and defence lawyers. I was gob smacked. What was happening? It was clear. We stopped you, you were disqualified, and you attacked us both. When it came out that he was already on license, it became clearer. If found guilty, he would have been back inside for a long time.

Several hours passed before we were told nearly all the offences were to be dropped, including the assaults on John and I. They had struck a deal. The story he gave was of his fear that he was being chased by dangerous people and was desperate to get to somewhere safe. He swore that at no time did he hear, 'Stop Police, you are under arrest.' He thought he was being attacked and did everything he could to protect himself. What a load of bollocks. It just stinks, but this is why barristers get 'silly money' to wear daft wigs. Me, I just drove a traffic car and gave out tickets.

They'd found and used loopholes in statements cross-referenced with CCTV, down to every minuscule detail. He ended up back in prison but for much minor offences like no insurance and car tax. I would have preferred to drop all of that and just seen him brought up on the assault charges or for resisting arrest, but there was no official action taken for these; we hadn't had the time to make our report accurately enough. He evaded the more serious accusations.

What effect does that have on me? I think I would be better off being a machine. It wouldn't sting so much then. I wear my uniform, go out and protect people, always doing the correct thing because I have sworn an oath to the Queen. For what? To be made to look a liar and stupid or be told 'you are a liar and no good'.

Until the day I retired, The DS and I never spoke again. He would walk past me and not make eye contact. I knew I had shown disrespect for a supervisor, but I was being treated like a six-year-old child, even though I had been ordered to make a statement which should have waited. A year after the event, I still suffered from a click when I coughed, and my chest remained tender to the touch. Had I broken some of my ribs? I can't say. I didn't receive any medical treatment; I was too busy writing a report.

Was I sorry I had lost my temper, become human? No, I wasn't I knew fully that in every situation I must remain neutral, must not take any sides. Only the facts mattered. The facts would have been accurate had I not been injured and hurting. I had deserved better treatment. Until that time, I hadn't ever been disrespectful. I was the officer who, even on my rest days, continued being an officer of the law.

Hadn't I bulled my boots until I could see my face in them? Wasn't my uniform always smart? Weren't my outer jackets and fleeces cleaned, my haircut and facial hair just so? Sorry I slipped up and stopped being a machine for a moment in time. Even the best machines crack, break or fail.

What do you expect when you have pushed us to the very depths of our limits? Did I know my limits? Of course not. No one does until we reach them. I reached mine, and they judged me for it; criminalised for my failings, which could have been avoided. All it would have taken was a friendly word; a caring arm, a smattering of advice warmly given.

You can have the newest, fastest, best self-drive car in the world and it will still have its faults. The manufacturer will get straight on the case and address the issue in a timely way. It will thank them with excellent service. I didn't get that chance.

The work I did was always done to the best of my ability. Whether in machine mode or reverting to my human instincts, I did all I could to do my job to the highest level. I hope that is what I am remembered for and not my failings.

Chapter 7- My Head Hurts

November 2011, I'm at the top of my game. I'm in traffic, I love my job. It's a cold October. I leave Toller Lane Police Station. I'm in my pursuit vehicle and I'm on my way to go hunting for the 'dark shadows' of society; criminals who think they can use the roads as racetracks, deal drugs and burgle houses. These are my primary targets.

I hope that by the end of my duty I'll be coming back, having made multiple arrests, given out tickets and made seizures. I, along with my colleagues, would compete to see who had the most successful day. The competitive element meant we made a massive impact on the roads of Bradford.

I was in a great place, mentally and physically, and had the respect of my team members. The car I drove was classed as a 'Subaru catcher' and was a monster on the road. It was a V6 Vectra VXR, my pride and joy; I named her Christine. She was like my baby.

I remember it was an early shift. I was out in the Heaton area of Bradford. Christine was shining like a new pin, and I was proud. I had just dropped on a 'no insurance' driver on Duckworth Lane. The car I pulled up stood out like a shed on wheels, and I got the same old story I'd heard many times before: 'Sorry Officer I was going to get insured, but I forgot.' I had no sympathy the first time I heard the excuse, and I have none now.

If I have to insure my car, so does everyone else. Anyway, the car was seized, and we prosecuted the driver. We had a great working relationship with 'McAdams Vehicle Recovery' and always enjoyed chatting to the drivers. So, I'm standing chewing the fat and getting the usual abuse from the young lads who are driving around the area, feeling big in their parents' Audi RS3 or an AMG Mercedes.

I then hear over my police radio. 'Can you have traffic, 1965? Are you free for this pursuit?' I didn't know at the time that there was a Ford Transit van failing to stop in the Barkerend area of Bradford. It was being pursued by a beat car. I wasn't far away, so ran to my faithful Christine, clicked on the seat belt and floored it in first gear. I loved the power of that car, the sound of the V6 roaring along the road, her turbo whistling; It was fantastic.

I turned down Toller Lane and left onto Carlisle Road, a quicker drive and easier at midday. In front of me was the usual deaf driver who couldn't hear sirens and doesn't look in his mirror. I passed him in a controlled manner, as taught to me at Crofton. I used all the skills I learned and knew that in a short time I would be in the pursuit.

As I approached the junction of Manningham Lane, the traffic was light; I braked smoothly up to the junction. Looking left and right with nothing coming, I cautiously went through and was soon driving down Queen's Road, heading for Canal Road. Queen's Road is a wide, single carriageway with stone terraced houses on either side. At the end is a crossroads junction. The approach lights were on red, so I knew I needed to use caution. I might be in a police car, but I still have to manoeuvre safely when travelling at speed. I slowed my speed to 15 mph. The driver coming in the opposite direction flashed his lights, so he saw me. Using normal practice, I crossed into the opposite carriageway to take control of the road.

A car came from my right; I got a 'thank you' wave from the driver, so I knew I was safe to continue. I looked to my left and saw a large Ford Transit van come to a stop. The driver gave me a 'thumbs up.' Okay, I knew I was safe in all directions. I pushed the throttle down and accelerated off hard through the junction. I was almost through, and just half a mile from the pursuit when - 'BANG'.

I was totally confused; I thought I'd driven over a bomb. Instantly, my torso, head and left arm were in the passenger seat, even though I was wearing my seat belt. White dust filled the car, and I could smell an intense burning. The sound of bending metal, skidding rubber and crunching filled my ears. I had never heard a sound like that.

Another instant and I was thrown back with a tremendous force into the driver's seat. It felt like a speeding train had hit me. I felt my head hit the 'A' section of the car, my entire body was wracked with pain and then total darkness and silence descended.

When I came round and opened my eyes, my head and chest were leaning on the steering wheel. The horn was beeping. Through bleary eyes I looked out of the front windscreen. The car bonnet was embedded in some steel railings and a lamp post. As I struggled to focus, I smelled burning. I knew it was coming from the side impact airbags, filling the car.

I tried to move, but I was held down. I tried harder but it was futile. I also realised I couldn't hear a thing other than the loud whistling and ringing in my ears. I managed to lean forward and push the yellow button on my radio. I mumble, 'CRASH, CRASH, CRASH.' This results in panic in the control room. They have heard it but can't see a thing. All types of scenarios would run through their heads as they tried to get CCTV to show something. Panic and pain set in for me, as I struggled to pull myself out of the car, unaware that the seat belt was still fastened and holding me in. I thought, 'I'm paralysed.' Everything was surreal. I felt I was in a dream and couldn't wake up.

Down the road, officers in a 'plain-clothes CID car,' had heard the collision over their radio but couldn't see it. By then, traffic was backing up and people were running across the road to investigate. Officers from the other car saw my wrecked traffic car, so they radioed ahead, gave the correct location and called for help.

What happened next, I don't remember fully. I know they extracted me from the car and put me on a spinal board. I also know it terrified me, but apparently all I could ask them was how was Christine, my baby? This caused panic. They thought a child had been in the car and were looking for her. They were asking me if there were other people, and I couldn't answer; I was stuttering so badly. I wanted to tell them there was no baby, but nothing I was saying made any sense.

I know someone took my radio off me because they didn't want me to go to hospital with my gear on me. They knew that if I had to go to theatre, it could go missing and then there could be a real problem.

Fortunately, a paramedic who knew me, arrived on the scene. He was able to give my details. I had worked with him before at several accident scenes, so we knew each other well.

Next, I knew, I was being 'blue lighted' to hospital. By the time we got there, my hearing had returned to normal. The stuttering was getting worse, but I felt I was talking the same as usual. To everyone listening it was like an old VHS video recorder that skipped every time 'play' was pressed. The words just wouldn't come out of my mouth. I was also struggling to grab my left hand, which was randomly pointing around the room as if it had a mind of its own.

Now if you think this would prompt any compassion from my colleagues, think again. Unless you are missing a major body part, you get no sympathy at all from fellow emergency workers. They see police officers brought into casualty all the time. They see us as fixtures and fittings. I know several of the doctors and nurses by their first names.

As soon as the doctor had done his initial assessment, with me still on the spinal board, my neck held in place by a brace, the nurse walks in, grinning from ear to ear. 'Hi Ben, what have you been doing? Head injury, is it? Right then, let's get your pants off.' This happened to me every time I arrived in casualty and couldn't move. It gave my colleagues and medical staff alike a good laugh.

There had been no examination of my hips, knees or ankles by the time Milly arrived. She later told me she had been waiting for me when I came out of the ambulance. I wasn't aware of this. It was her, however, who asked the doctors why I was stuttering, and told them this wasn't normal for me.

For several hours they prodded, poked and scanned me. They then released me into Milly's care because I wouldn't let them keep me in for observations. They had found nothing abnormal, so I didn't want to waste their time. They explained to me that the impact had been so great on my brain it had literally fried my circuits. That was why I couldn't grip correctly and was stuttering.

I had been unconscious for a brief period in the car and, whether because of drugs or my head being banged hard, my grasp of reality was confused. I could recall some things, but not others. If I'd known that I was actually poorly, I wouldn't have insisted on going home. I had been thrown around like a rag doll, but I didn't know how much I had been damaged.

I could only leave because they saw Milly as a responsible bobby, but they weren't thrilled when I signed myself out. I did, or Milly, I can't remember which of us signed the paper, but I knew she would take care of me.

I returned a few days later for more tests and scans. I was battered and bruised, and my speech was getting worse. I could hardly walk and needed help to get dressed. My back, my neck, everything hurt. I couldn't bend or stand properly. It was like I had a full body whiplash rather than just a neck injury. I had a massive, purple bruise across my chest and stomach where the seatbelt had forced me back into my seat from the passenger seat.

Over the days, my confusion also grew. I was finding it hard to do things with my left hand; simple actions like holding a pen. I'm left-handed, so that was really scaring me. I then found myself bounced from one hospital to another. I saw specialist after specialist and underwent a constant barrage of scans and memory tests.

I'm trying to cope with the distress of the accident, when I am informed by my sergeant that I'm under investigation for driving without due care and attention. I still don't know what's going on in my body or my brain. Will I ever walk properly again or gain full use of my left-hand side? Is my life changing for ever? I can't drive. It was three weeks before I could walk 250 metres.

Milly was having to do everything: shower me, bath me, dry me, put my pyjamas on. I didn't feel like a man anymore. I was terrified, I have to tell you that. I'd heard about people like Sylvester Stallone who had strokes. It changed the way they spoke and their physical features. I knew a friend who had 'Bell's Palsy.' He couldn't talk, dribbled all the time, and I admit, initially, I thought it was funny. How much I regret that.

Now I was on the other side and knew what he had gone through.

I was dribbling saliva down my chest. People I met thought I was drunk or ignorant. If I drank a juice, it would spill all over my shirt. It wasn't my lips; I just had no co-ordination at all. My speech deteriorated. It sounded like I just couldn't be bothered to talk. Milly would take the piss out of me. That didn't upset me, but the thought that people would feel sorry for me did.

I had always seen myself as trendy, one of the top lads in any group. Suddenly, I could see myself being pitied, and it really got to me. About a month after the crash, we were at Morrison's and met a girl we knew. She couldn't believe it was me. I was hunched over because my back was still bad. I was slurring when I talked. The look on her face said everything.

The doctor explained to me that my brain was like a filing cabinet that had tipped over. Everything had spilled out and been put back in the wrong order. It would time for it to be sorted into the right sections again.

It didn't stop me feeling ashamed, though. I felt everyone was looking at me. I was like an adult baby who couldn't function. I couldn't even sign my name, yet I was only in my thirties. I became withdrawn and didn't want visitors to call and see me. I couldn't drive or ride my motor bike. It had stopped all the things I loved doing without warning. I wasn't prepared; I wasn't old and worst of all, I caused it myself. I had made a simple mistake. I hadn't realised it was a two-lane carriageway. I had failed to see the black Vauxhall Corsa until it smashed into the side of my car.

I had no excuse; I was an advanced driver and should have seen the Corsa approaching. It was a minor error of judgement on my part that would leave a massive trail of destruction in its wake. The investigation would be thorough, they could prosecute me. Everything was unravelling before my eyes.

I worried what my colleagues would say if I lost my job. I didn't want to end up being the joker that crashed his car. I have always tried to be the best I can be and never thought I would end up in an investigation and lose everything; my reputation as a good bobby, erased by one mistaken judgement. I was lucky I didn't get taken to court. I had to go on a refresher driving course. I was humiliated, but at least I saved something. I passed and gained some credibility again.

My health concerned me, I had a head injury confirmed by several brain specialists, and I didn't know if I was every going to recover. For six months a woman came to my house to give me speech therapy. It comprised memory tests and exercises to get my brain working again.

Even now I can't write properly, I write like a seven-year-old. I remember when Pat, my friend and the co-author of this book, asked me to write out my thoughts. She quickly changed her mind and told me I would be better typing them out. 'Your writing is shocking,' she told me. We laughed about it, but it made me realise that even now, ten years later, I have still a way to go.

How much the accident had affected me, I didn't know. I often wondered at the time why Milly would want to stay with me. I hadn't been with her long and here she was looking after an invalid. We were fortunate, since it developed a close bond between us. I had to trust her, and she had to trust and hope that I would get better. None of us knew what the outcome would be.

This was the start of my C-PTSD. But to end this chapter on a lighter note, there was a funny side to it. I was working a night shift and was locking up a driver for being over the limit. I requested him to provide a sample. I was so tired that my voice was slurred, and I was dribbling. He asked me who was more drunk, him or me? On returning the prisoner to the station, I was more embarrassed when the custody sergeant asked if I was drunk on duty, and I had to be breathalysed in front of him because I looked and acted like I was pissed.

On a serious note: Never would it have entered my head that the trauma of the crash would be the start of the biggest nightmare I would ever face. My diagnosis with C-PTSD.

Until you have had a terrible collision, you can never comprehend how it messes with your mind and your body. On a scale of one to ten, mine was a horrendous collision I would definitely give an eight to. You can understand my pure anger when I see people run off from accident scenes, leaving the injured unattended, all to save their own skin, even if it means someone else may die. How appalling is that? How can you sleep at night knowing you left someone to die?

Human nature is to be loved, cared for, and show compassion to others. If you were on a desert island, alone and isolated, you would go mad, because the basic needs of humanity would be absent. Knowing someone is there for you is a massive comfort. Hearing a gentle voice, being aware you are not alone. It means so much when you need help because you are hurt. How can someone run? Why?
If you have caused an accident, or committed another crime, you might be prosecuted, but you would still have your self respect if you stood up to it. You would if it was your mother, or a close family member, and you would expect someone else to do the same. When you are standing at the roadside with an injured person, you can feel their fear. They are so scared, and what do they see? A coward running away with no compassion, leaving them in their moment of despair; heart-breaking.

I was fortunate it was daylight and people were about. Colleagues and emergency workers soon assisted me. I think how different it might have been, had I been injured on a lonely road at night. I have seen so many accidents where the offender has done a runner, and it never ceases to amaze me that people can do that. I know I couldn't.

Chapter 8 – I. O. D's

Whilst the head injury I suffered in the crash was probably the worst accident I ever had in the police force, it was one of many; hundreds, to be exact. I may be only 44 years of age, but sometimes I feel double that. I am slower and more worn from the battering my body has taken than a normal 44-year-old would be.

I get out of bed in a morning and sound like a creaking gate. My bones ache, my muscles and joints are stiff. My body has so many scars it resembles a roadmap. Part of it I attribute to sitting hours on end in a police car, without exercise but keeping my mind alert enough to go into action at a moment's notice. My body isn't warmed up but it doesn't mean I'm not ready to sprint from my vehicle, and chase a criminal down with a full kit weighing an extra stone or two. I have to be fit, it's my job to be ready.

It can require me to race across muddy fields, jump fences, scale a wall to catch a criminal, who may then drag me across concrete, my knees scraping as I try to regain my footing. This is a constant for me, day in, day out, week after week. Is it surprising that I now struggle to get out of bed?

Nobody should have to live with the constant threat of injury. Police officers do. The scars remain as a reminder of the physical damage done. The mental and emotional damage remains hidden. Each scar tells a story, a tale of a pursuit, a foot chase or fight. My kids hold my hands and ask me how I got the marks, and will they get the same marks on their hands? I tell them the stories, but without the grim details. I am constantly reassuring them that daddy is fine and will always be there with them.

I could tell them that my scars are small compared with some colleagues. I know of officers who have fallen from roofs, taken rides on car bonnets, or received such a bad beating it left them battered black and blue. Each one has to log off work and go home to their waiting families, who then also face the pain of their loved ones being hurt.

I can't recall the number of times Milly has had to meet me at the hospital, then explain to the kids why daddy's hand is bandaged or why he is limping. So how do these injuries occur? Let me tell you about just a few of them.

I was on patrol with my oppo in Shipley. It was around 11pm and fairly quiet; a boring night really, until our 'in-car ANPR system' alerted us to a vehicle being driven by a driver with no license or insurance. Spotting us, the car took off. We chased it around Shipley for a good twelve minutes. It was a great pursuit. No matter what he did, he couldn't shake us. Left, left, left, right, right, right at speeds of 90 mph. The roads were dry, and all was going well until I got complacent.

We continued down a minor road until the car turned right and came to an abrupt stop. He was going to throw his car into reverse, and I recognised this. He was preparing to ram us. I tried to put the BMW 330 into reverse, but because I had braked so sharply, it wouldn't select the gear. My oppo and I were both sitting there looking at the offender in an old pool car. It was as if we were in slow motion as he selected his gear, reversing at over 20 mph towards my shiny traffic car.

BANG - within seconds, we were thrown towards the dashboard. The Audi was ramming us. The front of our car took the force, the bonnet flew up; steam bellowed out of the engine. The car was destroyed. 'You Mother Fucker,' I screamed. With the car still in gear, I floored the 3-litre turbo engine, accelerated hard, ramming the Audi, pushing it up the street. Now, before you shout out or moan, there are reasons we do that.

He'd already rammed us, so I needed to close the gap between his car and ours to stop him doing it again. My car was going to pack up soon, so there was limited time to get this guy off the road. I couldn't cause any further damage to my car, so it was essential to stop his car and arrest him.

100 metres up the road, my car died on us. The Audi drove off into the distance, pursued by another traffic car. He crashed his car into trees a short time later and fled on foot.

Our battered car now stood stricken in the middle of the road. It was then I got a very uncomfortable feeling in my groin and lower back area. It felt as if someone with a needle was stabbing a pressure point, but I couldn't tell where it was.

I got out of the steaming car with a real urge to pee. It had come on suddenly, and if I didn't get somewhere fast, I knew I would piss myself. I ran to a small wall, jumped it, and urinated as though I had drunk ten pints of water. The pain went stratospheric; my knees buckled, I felt sick and was burning up. I staggered back to the car. My oppo knew something was wrong and could see I was struggling. The pain was getting worse and worse, and I was leaning on the car for support, trying to get my balance.

I knew something was seriously wrong, so-called over the radio for an ambulance. The feeling in my lower body was something else. I felt I wanted to defecate. My bowels and bladder were acting as if they had burst. I was clinging on, praying for some miracle to happen, only to find that an ambulance wasn't available for the next thirty to forty minutes. To my relief, a sergeant pulled up in her beat car.

'Get in, I'll run you to hospital. We'll get there fast,' she reassured me.

I dragged my injured body into the car, and we headed to the local accident and emergency department. In a police car, I knew we could 'blue light' it and would be there in minutes. It wasn't meant to be. I liked the driver, but 'blue light' means just that; drive as fast as it is safe to do so, before I died. She didn't, and remained at, and even below, the speed limits. We joined the dual carriageway, sirens and lights blaring. A 44-tonne goods vehicle overtook us; a man on a pedal bicycle could have overtaken us; cars were waiting to overtake us. I just wanted her to pull up and let me get into one of the passing cars.

The collision scene was only eight miles from the hospital, but at the rate we were going, I wasn't going to get there any time soon.

It should have taken us four or five minutes at most to get to the hospital with blue lights on. It took us the best part of twenty minutes. She is great police officer but couldn't drive for toffee.

In 'casualty,' I was examined and pumped full of morphine. I gave a urine sample and almost collapsed; it was a dark red liquid with bits of skin or flesh floating in it. I lay in 'casualty' for the next two hours in shock, while they conducted various tests. I was then told that the stent I had fitted because I have kidney stones, had dislodged and was causing me to bleed internally.

I also had a bulging disc in my lower back, just above the slipped disc I already had. My kidneys and bowels were bruised, caused by the speed of the forward motion of my body jolting against the seatbelt at the point of impact. The dipshit had wrecked both the car and me at the same time. I remained in hospital for three days.

I'd pissed out a kidney stone in excruciating pain, slipped a disc in my back, and displaced the disc above it. I'd dislodged my stent and displaced my hip all in one smash, only to be told by the doctor that I shouldn't have been working with a stent fitted in the first place. I was then placed on the ward with an elderly man in the bed next to me. He was a grumpy old git. They'd tell him to put his identity wristband on and he'd shout abuse left, right and centre. He told a Philippine nurse she was a black bastard and to fuck off home. I laid there, still in my uniform, curled up in a ball, waiting for my hospital gown, when he picked up his walking stick and waved it at the staff. All I wanted was to go somewhere else, pull the covers over my head and wait for the pain to stop.

The old man was threatening everyone in sight; I think there were about seven nurses, doctors and security staff around his bed not knowing what to do. I had to stand up and help them out. I'd blood on my boxer shorts; I was discharging fluid all over and now I was really pissed. I couldn't stand up straight because of my lower back injuries, so I hunched over because of the displaced hip. My 'Long John Silver' peg leg swung to the side, and I had to disarm an 80-year-old bloke called Errol to stop him bashing all the nurses with his walking stick. I grabbed his stick, threw it across at a wall, told him to shut up and show some god damn respect. The ward fell silent, with all the nurses and staff shocked at what they had just witnessed, I just crawled back into bed and fell asleep.

I don't think for one minute that I am alone in this. I recall a lad I was tutoring. His name was Andy. He had the nickname of 'preppy' because he was a posh lad and tight as a duck's arse. He would turn up for a pint wearing a nice pair of chinos, and a jumper across his shoulders. He had a heart of gold, but a wallet fastened with superglue.

There was a time when we were called out to a 'domestic'. Andy hadn't been in the force long, but this job was something and nothing. Two pissed men were being loud at the end of a night out. The partner of one man had phoned us because they wouldn't leave the house so she could go to bed. We arrived and asked them to leave, which they did with no fuss, no moans, nothing. 'Job done,' or so we thought. As we headed back to our car, we heard one of them say, 'I think we can take them.' We turn to see 'stupid one', and 'stupid two' walking towards our car. We just couldn't believe it; it was a simple job, which had become complicated in seconds.

The biggest of the two decided he could take me, leaving the small one to go for Andy. My assailant was like a big ape man with a smug grin on his face, but he was no Mohammed

Ali, more of a Mickey Mouse. He couldn't have pulled the skin off custard. The man about to attack Andy, however, was built like a brick shit house and fought like a 'pit-bull.' Within seconds, mine tasted the tarmac and was cuffed at the rear, but I couldn't leave him. You have a duty of care to look after your prisoner. 40 metres away, Andy was grappling with the pit-bull. They were knocking the stuffing out of each other, and I could hear the air leaving their bodies with each landed blow. It was like watching someone hitting a puppy in a bag.

I had no other option. I pressed my 'Code 0' button for urgent assistance. I had to stay with my prisoner, but Andy needed help. 'Don't give up,' I shouted to Andy, as he gasped between punches, 'I won't.' he replied. The guy then swings him sideways by his vest, lifting him off his feet. As Andy hit the tarmac, his cuffs and baton dropped from his belt and landed on the floor. Andy got up and charged the ape-man, his face full of rage. Punches and kicks were landed. It was like watching a low budget martial arts movie. Again, the man grabbed Andy by his stab vest and spun him 180 degrees and released him. He skidded across the wet tarmac, his stab vest hanging from him. Andy, now covered in marks and bruises, looked beaten. I heard sirens. Help was on its way. 'Fuck this,' I said to myself, 'you are not hurting my preppy.'

I stood up, leaving my gormless prisoner on the floor. Quickly, I ran over and landed a left hook on the pit-bull's jaw. It was just enough to stun him. Andy piled in with a full rugby tackle, taking him to the floor. I ran back to my prisoner who was just about to get up. We detained both men just as help arrived, and the pit-bull was finally restrained. We threw both him and the ape into the back of a transit van and escorted them to the cells. We charged both with assaulting a PC and resisting arrest.

Back at the station, we cleaned ourselves up before debriefing the job with the sergeant and the inspector. My admiration for Andy had grown immensely. I knew he was scared at the scene, but he wouldn't give up. The man was a real fighter and Andy, although in pain, was a Pimm's drinking lion; smaller and weaker in size and stature, but more courageous than anyone I have ever seen. Andy lives down South now and is still a police officer and close friend to this day. I truly miss working with him.

On another occasion there were two cars driven in the Bolton Woods area of Bradford; they were being followed by the owner as one was a stolen vehicle. Anyway, they went up a road and turned into a left-hand estate, a dead end with only one way out. So, me and my oppo John, travelling at some speed in order to get there, are having a laugh. We are talking about this being a simple job to end the day. It's going to be a simple box-in, then we're finished and home in time for supper.

We then heard over the radio that the culprits who were being followed have stolen a flatbed Transit laden with barrier railings; the type of railings used at concerts for crown control. We're informed it's in convoy with a silver Seat, also stolen. We are told that these three cars are all going to be together. We have no concerns as we are heading to the scene, the more stolen cars, the merrier. We're thinking it's going to be a piece of piss to stop and arrest them. We'll get some lock ups, hand it over and get off home. It had been a long shift and I'm only human. I wanted to get some rest.

So, we were flying up Livingstone Road, Bradford at about 60/70 mph in a 30 zone. We could see some beat cars behind us, who had joined the convoy. Suddenly, a Seat came out at the top of the road and eyeballed us. Effectively, he looked down on us; cars were parked on either side of the road, so there was only room for our two tonne BMW X5, and three quarters of a car gap. The criminals set off at speed, wheels spinning, and I could see they were wearing black balaclavas. The Seat headed straight towards me at speed. In my head I shouted 'fuck' I knew this was going to hurt.

It then became a game of 'let's play chicken.' A beat car veered out from the corner, only just missed my car, and got through the little gap. At the same moment, the stolen Transit van skidded around the corner, fully laden with its cargo. 'For fuck's sake,' I shouted, 'we need to stop one of these before someone gets really hurt.' It was like an episode of 'It's a Knockout', between the police and the thieving scum of society. It was just a matter of who had the most bottle. So, I slowed my speed down and braced for impact, but for some stupid reason the driver of the Transit thought he could do a handbrake turn to block our path. He aimed his van between our X5, into the small gap between the parked cars. He failed; he smashed into the stationary cars, then into the front of our police car. The bonnet of our X5 flew up and the wings crumpled. The barriers on the van propelled themselves over the bonnet and hit our windscreen. We came to a violent halt. I screamed as I shielded my face, thinking the window had come through. The noise of the metal crashing over the bonnet was horrendous. I didn't fancy my face being taken out, so I got my hands up over it as I hit the steering wheel. My foot was hard down on the brake, so the force of the impact shot up my thigh, and into my hip, displacing it.

I looked up to see these lads jumping out of the van and running past me smiling. I was incensed and thought, 'no way are you bastards getting away.' I opened the car door, adrenaline pumping, and set off after the suspects. Now I want you to imagine this: Think of Long John Silver trying to run with his peg leg. Well, that was me. One of my legs was going in front whilst the other looked like it was having a spasm behind me. I ran as fast as I could but couldn't understand why they were getting away. I'm a really quick runner; I should have been closing the gap.

To add insult to injury, this ginger-haired van driver was fat. Anyone could have caught him. My 90-year-old granny could have got him, but not me. In the end, I could only turn and go back up the hill. Well, I thought I could. As I approached my partner, John, I realised I couldn't walk. Panic set in. Had I broken my hip or my leg?

I started limping then and slowly hobbled back up the hill. By the time I got to the car I was sweating, I had pins and needles in my leg and hands. I felt as if I was on a merry-go-round with nausea. The pain was really starting up, and I saw there was a difference in the length of my lower legs. It was like someone had shaved a half inch off the right one.

A sergeant then turned up and I went straight to the GP, leaving our fucked-up car behind. My leg wasn't broken, and the doctor explained how simple it is to get this type of injury. You can displace your hip by stepping hard off a curb edge. Next thing I knew, I was in 'physio,' and an osteopath was assessing me. He told me I was a mess. My back was leaning one way, my leg the other. He asked if I'd been involved in any other accidents. It was hard to wipe the smile off my face when I told him 'I've been hurt a lot.' It turned out that the car I drive has the pedals off-set and causes many of these kinds of injuries to the hips and lower back.

I did exactly the same when faced with another balaclava wearing lad in a stolen car, heading towards me. I pushed my foot hard on the pedal and displaced my hip again when both cars made contact. Four lads ran from the car, all wearing balaclavas, and tried to make off. I chased them and tackled the driver; you always go for the driver first and get them cuffed. But when I tried to stand up, I couldn't walk straight. I knew exactly what had happened. It then made me very wary whenever I drove that type of car and knew I had to make contact, because I knew I could repeat this injury. I just have to live with that now.

Trust me, you don't want it to happen to you, it's so painful when they manipulate it back. You can hear it snap into place. I wouldn't mind, but the first time I did it I thought I had broken my leg and would get some kudos from the other officers. It wasn't so. If anyone can get it stepping off a curb, I was unlikely to get any sympathy at all, and I didn't. In the police force you have to be badly hurt before anyone takes notice and offers you commiserations.

As I said in 'Handcuffed Emotions,' you only have one body. Most people only have one or two accidents in a lifetime, but we experience them two and three times a week. Our bodies are not warmed up and nicely prepared when we have to run after a suspect. We don't get a nice long convalescence before going back into the field. This is day after day, week after week. More often than not, our injuries haven't healed correctly before it happens again. There is no reflection time to look at what happened, no 'physio' standing by to treat us. We live every day with our injuries. The impact on our bodies is horrendous in the long term. By the time I reached 40, I was like an old man trying to get up in a morning.

One of the most unbelievable accidents came when I applied for Christmas off work, and they wouldn't agree as we are usually busy. I threw my teddy out of the cot, left the sergeant's office, and headed out on patrol. I sat with a female police officer in one of our worst traffic cars. It Just wouldn't do what was expected of it. It was slow, handled badly, and shook under braking. We were parked up at the bottom of Baildon, watching the flow of traffic, when a stolen car announcement sounds on the radio. It's just been stolen and is speeding down the road towards our location, we're told. We are in the 'loner' car that no one wants to use. I couldn't have picked a worse vehicle for a high-speed pursuit. John my tutor, and an officer called Mark, are in the big VXR; the big powerful car that everyone wants and is just like my baby, Christine.

The stolen car shoots out right in front of us. Two Asian lads are in it, and we are 'game on.' I'm accelerating the loner car behind it but am struggling to keep pace. The car is making all sorts of sounds. It wouldn't surprise me if it fell apart as we hit the first speed bump. The exhaust is rattling, warning lights are coming on the dashboard; it's begging me to stop. I'm doing my best, but there's no way I can catch up in this crappy vehicle.

I see in my rear-view mirror that John is coming up behind me at speed, so I know there is no way the car we're pursuing is getting away. So, we continue to follow it down to the bottom of the Barkerend Road area. The driver does a hard left, then either stalls the car or runs out of petrol; I'm not sure, but it stops. John boxes it in at the back. We go around and block it to the front. I then see an Asian lad running past my car and legging it up the road. I throw open my car door and I'm in a foot pursuit. I'm fit and a runner, so he will not get away from me. I'm round my bonnet; I've gone into Terminator mode and I'm sprinting across the road. Suddenly, I'm moving at super speed. I'm like the bionic man; from seven miles per hour to 15 miles per hour. I'm moving faster and faster and then I realise I'm actually sitting on the front bonnet of the Vectra. John has hit me from behind; he just didn't see me there in the road. I feel myself go up in the air and then back, rolling across the bonnet of the car towards the floor. All sorts of shit is going through my mind. Will I be dead in four minutes? Will it drag me up the road under a car?

I can see the floor approaching really fast as I hit the tarmac and roll. All I can see is black sky, tarmac, engine sump, as I roll over and over, with the sump getting closer and closer to my head with each roll. I can see the wheel inches from my head. The heat is gushing down from the car engine. I hear the fan kick in to cool the engine down. I can smell burning oil at the bottom of the sump. I hear the tyres squealing as the car is skidding along the tarmac trying to come to a stop. I know I've gone under it and I think, 'that's it,' it's going to run me over.'

As I roll for the last time, my knee goes down and projects me back to my feet. I set off running again. Now, normally when I run, I see both hands, swinging in front of me, but this time all I could see was my left hand moving. I'm wondering where my right hand has gone. I look down and it's pinned across my body. I've only gone and broken my bloody elbow. I continue running for a bit before I feel strange. I stop, I'm in the middle of the road, and the adrenaline immediately stops pumping. I'm feeling very unwell, very quickly; everything is in slow motion. I feel like I'm in pixie land. The reality is I'm going into shock and in danger of passing out.

I sit down on the edge of the curb; everything is silent. The usual 'Fucking get him,' 'slap, slap, slap' and sirens blaring aren't there. I try to touch my arm and wince in pain. I lay down on my back; I see I've ripped my pants. My knees are bloodied. I stare at the clear night sky, counting the stars in the hope the pain will go away. Someone stands over me and asks, 'Ey up Benny boy, you alright?' I can remember saying, 'No....' I'm told not to worry; an ambulance is on its way.

Moments later I'm placed in the ambulance's rear and some bright spark says, 'We'll cut your stab vest off and get a better look.' Well, 'NO.... It's a stab vest, you will not cut it off.' 'These scissors go through everything lad.' 'NO.... It's a stab vest,' I repeat to a confused paramedic. So now they have to take it off. They unzip it and pull it over my broken arm. I scream in pain. John, who is still sitting down the road in the police car, radio bleeping and really upset that he's run me over, told me later that he could hear me screaming. He said it went through him; it was blood-curdling.

At the hospital, the paramedic relays my suspected injuries. 'This is Ben, he's done this and done that. His stats are etc. etc.' 'Right okay, let's take his pants off,' says the nurse. 'Here we are again,' I think to myself. I'm laid there, police uniform at the top half, with no pants on the bottom, bland boxer shorts and knees with skin ripped off. I'm off my rocker, pumped full of medication. Then in walks my sergeant and says, 'Now then you clot, what have you done?' No sympathy at all; he was old school. 'How have you bloody done this, ya fool?' he adds. 'You just wanted Christmas off, didn't you? You'll fucking do 'owt to get Christmas off.'

I ended up with 7/8 weeks off with my arm in a sling. I couldn't do riot training after that because I couldn't hold the shield without pain running down my arm. Even leaning on my elbow now is painful. Every time I knock it, I feel sick, and this is 13 years later. I had unbelievable whiplash, bruising to my spine, kidneys, neck and shoulders. I couldn't look after myself for a month afterwards. I needed so much help it was embarrassing.

This happened in 2007, and John and I have a running joke. Whenever we are in the office and having banter, I always say to him. 'Well, what are you going to do then, mow me down?' He gets pissed off and replies,' I didn't run you down, you ran out in front of me.' This went on for a few weeks until he suggested we replay the footage and let the lads in the office decide. We played it back, and they all looked at him and started tutting. 'What have you done John? You've mowed down a fellow officer.'

It gutted John, but it's all part of the job. Now had it been a civilian there would have been a claim put in against him, but when you are a cop, it's taken as part of the role. I would never put a claim in against another officer and risk his career.

It was just an unfortunate set of circumstances. John was an excellent driver and a good copper. It's part of the everyday challenges you face daily. Nothing braces you for the challenges, but you know they will happen. A member of the public would just stay down if they were run over, but a bobby is so full of adrenaline, they can't do that. Like me, they will get up and run again. It's only when the adrenaline stops that they realise they are injured.

You find it the same if you've been in a nasty fight with a suspect. The adrenaline is flowing, and you think nothing about whether you may be injured. You just set out to control the situation and arrest the criminal. It's only when they are in the cells that you stop and feel your hands shaking. You can feel ruined, like a boxer who's been in a ring with a madman.

Sometimes I've shaken so much, I have thought I was having a heart attack. The blood is raging through your system, and you know you have to calm it down. When this happens over and over, it's not good for your body. You also question how many more chases you want to be involved in. How much more can you push your body?

I'll give you another example. This was in the newspapers and shown on the Interceptors' programme. It was a stolen ambulance, involved in a fatal incident. It was refusing to stop. It came over the radio that it's heading towards us. Are there any West Yorkshire Police who can give assistance?

There we are, flying towards Crosshills at the other side of Keighley. North Yorkshire Police are coming towards us, pursuing this ambulance. I'm driving hard, 110mph in a 30 zone. I'm switched on. Me and my oppo are talking about the fact that if this man has been involved in a fatal collision, he could already be a murderer. It's that simple. He is now heading for Keighley Town Centre at 4pm on a Friday afternoon. I shout up that if the vehicle comes towards us, we will use tactical contact to stop it. We can't let it pass us and get to Keighley and be responsible for him killing someone else.

As we come towards the Crossroads at Crosshills, the situation is getting intense. He's coming up the wrong side of the road and straight through the level crossing, smashing into it. He's then abandoned the ambulance and run away. A couple of seconds earlier and he would have derailed a train. Other officers had been trying to halt the train, but at 90 mph it can't stop immediately. There are ambulances everywhere, TV crews and police.

Had it not crashed when it did, Baby Ben and I would have been badly hurt because we would have had to stop it by ramming it to the front to push it away from the train track. It would have ruined our car, but we would have been committed to do it; to flip it on its roof. We may have killed the driver and ourselves. What do you do? Do you risk a train being derailed and dozens killed? Do you risk a nutcase ploughing people down on a busy afternoon in a town centre?

It wasn't until it was over that I sat in the car and realised that I was as near as I had ever been to leave my kids without a dad. I had made a choice to protect the public. I was sworn to protect the public, and it's a strange feeling when faced with a life-or-death situation. My oppo, Ben, and I, had consciously put our lives at risk to do our job; to protect strangers who wouldn't recognise us again if they saw us in the street.

You are just a face that blends into a crowd, nothing or nobody special until someone is hanging out of a crashed car or wielding a knife. You then stand to be counted. You step forward. It's a code that officers worldwide follow. It's written into their DNA. I'm not happy with the injuries I have received, but I'm not sad either. I learned from everyone, and I did my job well. It's part of my story. It's my life in the police force and I'm proud of it.

Chapter 9–Handcuffed Emotions, the Impact.

I look back and ask myself how it all started. What made me think I could produce a book as revealing about my mental health status as 'Handcuffed Emotions?' I'd been told that it would help with my recovery, but I never thought it would have the impact that it has, not just on my life, but also on the lives of many others.

It wasn't a straightforward process; it was a very painful one. I had to remember things I didn't really want to. My co-author, Pat Sutcliffe, pushed and poked to drag the information to come to the surface. I have said before about the hours we spent together working on the book. What I haven't told you about is the number of times it reduced me to tears in her company. Re-living the incident involving the young boy was gut wrenching to me, but I knew if the book was to be an honest account of the experiences that led to my C-PTSD, I had to put myself back there; replay it and tell it as it was.

Four months later, 'Handcuffed Emotions' emerged from its chrysalis. I had been ripped apart mentally, gone through hours of writing my memories, and it left me exhausted by the experience. I was torn about the release date. Initially, it was going to be in time for Christmas, but my Twitter followers pushed me to get it out earlier.

I was full of angst; I wasn't a writer, and I'm certainly no academic. I thought people would laugh at me and it would end up as one of those books you buy for 25p in the charity shop. This was something entirely new to me. I had no comfort zone I could use as a haven. I could only hope the book would touch the hearts of readers, and something good would come out of it.

My initial thoughts were for my family. What impact would it have on them? I also thought, stupidly, that people would think I wasn't ill if I could produce a book. I was afraid they would misunderstand my reasons for putting pen to paper and get the impression I had fielded a big money contact with a big publisher. Nothing could be further from the truth. I stood to gain nothing from the book other than self-healing. I wanted to show others they were not alone, and mental illness was not something that should be swept under the carpet.

For all my doubts, I admit one part of me was excited to see my story in print, but it terrified another side of me. I was laying myself bare. I suppose if I'm honest, my trust in people, from the experiences I had gone through, was at a low ebb. I don't think I even trusted myself, let alone the decisions I was making. But decide I did. The release date was set for November 21st, 2020.

The fear I felt was immense from the minute I pressed the publish button. There was no going back then. My story had already been published in the Telegraph & Argus, and to my surprise and shock, it had been front page news. A reporter, who said she wanted to run a story on my mental health struggle, had approached me. Now, normally, I wouldn't trust anyone to write things about me without checking what was being written. She was so easy to talk to though, I felt completely at ease with her. We had a long 'Zoom' session, and a week later the article appeared.

The response was very positive. Within seconds of the paper coming out, my Twitter and e-mail accounts were receiving posts from people thanking me for being me, and for speaking up about PTSD. I felt such love and support from individuals I didn't even know, I had never met, and probably would never see. This gave me that extra bit of confidence to push the button. Once it was done, that was it. There was no turning back.

I had choices, and I knew that. I could either become a loser, wallowing in self-pity, or create a future for myself and my family. I was feeling in charge of my own life. Milly always told me I needed to believe in myself more, rather than being so negative, but PTSD takes away your self-belief, and I knew I needed to find it again. Publishing my book was one way I could do that. It filled me with mixed emotions, and I was almost scared to turn on Amazon. It felt like Christmas; I had just unwrapped a big present but was scared it wasn't for me, and I would go to jail for stealing it.

Then, out of nowhere, I was contacted by someone who said they were a publicist. A what? I had no idea what a publicist was or did, let alone why one should contact me. She was a lovely lady and told me she worked with stars from TV and film. When she explained that the impact of my book could be beyond anything I could imagine, I didn't quite believe her. How wrong I was.

She was throwing me a lifeline in the choppy media sea; an arena that was alien to me. This lady with a kind heart was offering to guide and steer me through it. As an ex-bobby, my suspicious mind locked in. I wondered what she wanted in return. Was I going to be abused, taken for a ride or worse still, left to sink? We talked at length about what the future may hold, and I felt she was on the same wavelength as I was and could be completely trusted. So, my work with her began.

My publicist would deal with any media enquiries, bookings and interviews that came in from a media circus I knew existed, but never expected to be involved in. I was more than grateful for her help. Alone, I would have gone under for sure, not knowing what was happening, and I'd have become so confused I could have regressed rather than being healed.

I told her from the beginning that I wasn't running on full batteries and that there would, without a doubt, be times I couldn't do what was being asked of me. I wanted to help others as much as I could, but there would be times when I felt so poorly, I just needed to sleep. We agreed that if this happened, things would be re-arranged or simply cancelled. I felt so much better, but I was, in no way prepared for the aftermath of the book's publication.

The first of many interviews was with BBC Radio Leeds. They wanted me to talk about my journey and the book. I welcomed the opportunity; it was a chance to let a wider audience know it was okay to speak out. That was the start. It was like a snowball that grew and grew; the more I fed it, the bigger it grew. My publicist handled all the arrangements, and I was just told when, who and where. I cannot thank her enough for that, and I want her to know how much I appreciate her support.

The positivity overwhelmed me. It took away the pain from the few, who thought all I had been through, and was still going through, was some elaborate plot to leave my job with a hefty pension, and make millions through selling books, and becoming some sort of star. They had warned me about these types of people, but I didn't see why they would want to attack someone trying to help others speak out about mental health.

Such a person doesn't know I have to see a therapist every week and will do for a long time; the type of person who isn't aware of the nightmares I still have, the visions that I scream to forget but can't. There were those people I saw as friends, but now I realise with great sadness, I was just their colleague, nothing more. It hurts to read and hear some of the negative comments, but none of it will change my determination to get well again. I'm not a loser, I won't be a loser, and I won't let negative gossip make me into one.

When I read the comments on my Twitter account, and e-mails I received from people who also suffer from mental issues, I felt it was all worthwhile. When I now send a cheque for over a thousand pounds to charity, I know it's all worthwhile. From the minute I released the book, I received over 50 direct messages of support, thanks and praise from doctors, lawyers, firefighters, ambulance workers and members of the special forces, the world over, but also, and importantly, other police officers who were going through the same as I was.

I had opened a taboo subject that people wanted to talk about, and now they felt they could. High-ranking police commanders retired Chief Constables, MP's, celebrities were all sending their best wishes, some telling me about their own personal struggle. It was surreal, but I was so grateful to them.

As soon as my book hit the shelf, everything went stratospheric. 100's of messages per day. My social media was going mental. I had to keep pinching myself to understand. Newspaper after newspaper, radio station upon radio station, all wanted my story. Then I opened my computer and loaded Amazon. I had to do a double take. I screamed for Milly to come and look. 'Handcuffed Emotions' had shot to the bestseller list on 'Police Biographies.' We just cuddled each other; I couldn't believe it.

I knew I had made a difference; I had done something beneficial. I'd always put myself on the line as a police officer, but now I was putting myself on a different type of line; one for the entire world to see. I don't want to get to the pearly white gates and when St. Peter asks me about my life, say it stopped when I was 44 years old. I want to say, I suffered, I fought back, and I made a difference.

I can't work at the moment, I'm not mentally fit enough, but what I can do is talk and I can write. I remember the first day I met Pat, and she told me that there would be negativity, people wanting to trash what I was doing, but I had a choice to make; go ahead or fold, I went ahead. I remember reading the first part of the book and it was there in black and white, me baring my soul. It was a strange feeling. I could see and feel the pain even on the first pages. When reading the dedications, it reiterated why I had put my life into a book. If people don't like it, then don't read it. Leave it for those who are being helped by it. Or rather, continue reading it and think yourselves lucky that you don't know the pain of mental illness.

One request they asked of me, early on, was a podcast with two other police officers. One was the guy who had been on 'Britain's Got Talent' with Finn, the police dog who was stabbed; the other was a well-known podcaster and ex-firearms sergeant, a VIP protection officer. I enjoyed doing that because I was comfortable with men I saw as comrades. Bobbies like me. I was less comfortable with the radio interviews. I hadn't been used to doing things like that. I know I must have sounded like I was in a job interview on some. After a while, I realised, they gave me an opportunity to talk about mental health and get the 'It's okay to talk' message out.

I also made sure that everyone who had taken the time to contact me, irrespective of what media they had chosen, would receive a reply. I wouldn't turn down anyone wanting to talk. The more I got the message out, the more likelihood they would do something about the way mental illness was treated in organisations.

It was then that television stations became interested. They contacted me from 'Look North.' A lovely woman talked to me and told me how much my story resonated with her, and she thought I could do an interview on TV for greater awareness. Well, as most people know. TV isn't new to me. I jumped at the chance. The more people I could reach, the more I could help.

Another organisation that contacted me was 'Andy's Man Club.' I knew little about the club at the time; I thought it was like a counselling group, but I soon realised it wasn't. Its principal aim is to cut the number of suicides in men under the age of 45, and was set up by Luke Ambler, after his brother-in-law committed suicide. I also found out that there are over 40 'Andy's Man Clubs' around the country, offering support to men when they are at their lowest ebb.

I did a podcast with Luke, and it amazed me. The positive vibes he gave off as he walked into the room to talk to me were inspiring; his aura overpowered me. He was so kind, so heartfelt. I felt so comfortable; we just talked. He could have been my brother. I wear the tee shirt he gave me with pride and will do all I can to promote his organisation.

Doing podcasts took me into another world; another side of social media I had little understanding about. I have had to learn quickly, but learn I have. I have now done multiple video casts, which I release every Friday. They have been phenomenally successful. Josh, the production guy, is so knowledgeable with his finger on the pulse. He knows all there is to know about 'YouTube' and podcasts for other outlets, and he told me he couldn't believe how well the programmes have gone down.

In just over four months, the 'YouTube' channel has reached over 51,000 subscribers. The videos created have just short of 3.1 million views, and they are being shared worldwide. I'm now being contacted by some of the biggest 'You Tubers' in the U.K who want to chat and listen to my stories. I also have podcasts, live talks, motivational speaking events, plus many other things lined up; so, watch this space.

What's important to me, though, is that I do not lose sight of my original goal of reaching as many people as possible to get the message across that there is power in numbers. The more of us who speak out, the more will be done to recognise that mental health in the workplace is a serious problem. We need to tackle it head on.

Chapter 10–Life After the Badge

As I sit outside the office in my best uniform, my tunic and gleaming white gloves, I look down at my boots; they are bulled and shined to within an inch of my life. I can't describe the sadness and apprehension I feel. A soft lady's voice tells me they are ready to see me now.

My heart skips a beat, I take a deep breath as I push open the hand-carved doors. I admire the wood-panelled walls of the office. The top half is painted green, setting off the deep red carpet. The décor takes me back to 1920s New York. I imagine I'm in a millionaire businessman's office. I'm in line for some great bonus for work I have done for him.

Before me stands a man in a crisp uniform. I can see my reflection in his shoes. He holds out his hand to shake mine. The grip is firm; I know he is the big 'honcho,' my employer. 'Ben, hello, take a seat. 'I'm almost trembling as I sit down on the big leather couch. I hear cracking noises as I sink into its hide. I shuffle about trying to get comfortable; the chair makes funny noises as it welcomes me. I know I'm going to be here for a while.

'Tea with sugar, Ben?' His voice is assertive, authoritative.
'No sugar, sir.' My response is quick.

I'm handed a large china cup with the words 'West Yorkshire Police' printed on the side. I'm feeling something special is going to happen. I sip my tea slowly; I want to savour the moment. How often do I get to sit in a plush office? The boss smiles at me and offers me a biscuit. I take three; they can afford it. My sense of humour slips through. It's so strange; here I am with the hob-knobs, being offered 'hobnobs', although I would have preferred 'Jammy Dodgers'.

'Well, thank you Ben for coming in today, I'd just like to say a few words.'

He talks for 30 minutes about himself before moving onto my career. I listen with pride as he talks about the vast difference, I have made to crime in the Bradford area; how I am a role model, who is looked up to by officers and probationers alike. We chat, laugh, share jokes and sip tea. I feel so amazing. My 19 years on the force have been worth it. I'm loved and thanked by the top brass.

I'm then presented with a large certificate in a gilded frame. The inscription reads 'On Your Retirement, Dedicated Service, Loyal Officer.' I'm blown away. He then hands me another frame, a sunken one in which my collar number 1965 is mounted. Alongside, sit my medals and a mini truncheon. It's known as a plaque of honour. I feel my eyes well up with tears; I'm overcome with emotion. I don't know where I am going in the future, but I know I have made a big impression in police circles. The love shown to me by everyone is overwhelming.

I want to continue chatting, but there's tap, tapping on my shoulder and it is distracting me. 'Sorry, sir,' I hear myself saying. I'm getting pissed off now; the tapping is annoying me. I reach to scratch my shoulder; there's a little warm hand on it. 'Daddy, can we get up now? I open my eyes. My four-year-old son is standing by my bedside. The room is dark. I check my watch; it shows 06:42 hours. I want to cry. It was all a dream. No plush office, no brew, no certificate. No 'hobnobs' of any shape or size. The farewell I envisaged would be my last day was all in my mind.

The hard graft, the shifts, the injuries. Trauma upon trauma. Nineteen years of my life, for what? The thanks I felt due to me wasn't to be. My retirement wasn't a large display of gratitude; far from it. My days on the force ended with a telephone call I received from a friend when leaving the gym; Craig, a Federation Officer, who had supported me through thick and thin. He's such a nice bloke, but I could hear something different in his voice. He simply informed me that the police had retired me off. He apologised on their behalf and said I would hear something from them soon. I had expected a nicely drafted letter and an invitation to attend a special farewell. I received nothing other than this impersonal call. The bosses had simply made their decision, and I was gone. I could hear the conversation.

'Jenny, what are we going to do with Ben?'
'Let's just get shut, Bob.'
'Well, are we giving him anything for his 19 years' service?'
'Naa, just let him go.'
I see them press 'delete' on the system and I'm finished; ended, I never existed.

So now I don't just feel like I'm worthless, I know so. I've spent nineteen years making no contribution; I'm of no value. I feel like I'm falling over burning, but instead of being protected by the force, they throw more petrol over me and they're laughing at who is going to light the match. I'm left feeling depressed and worthless.

Two weeks later I am asked to attend headquarters to see a Chief Superintendent. I don't know him; I've never met him. He knows absolutely nothing about me. He's not a trusted friend, my old sergeant or my boss, Owen West, who was such a great man. I so wish it could have been him. But no, it's none of these. It was a total stranger. Milly and I faced the officer, who told me how sorry he was that I'd been failed. I will never forget his words. 'You've simple fallen through the cracks. "Fallen through the cracks.' What the fuck. Did he just admit that? I was fuming. I wanted to rip his head off. I was waiting for my turn to speak; all hell was about to be unleashed. The fury in me was raging; different scenarios ran through my head. I could see myself smashing the door down, only to be held down by six 'firearms officers.' If he hadn't been an officer of the law, I would have beaten him with a rubber hose and made him beg for mercy. 'Fallen through the cracks;' what a fucking insult.

He asked if there was anything I would like to say. I looked at Milly; she smiled and gave me a friendly nod. This man meant nothing to me; his rank, his badges, nothing. They had broken me, and he wanted to know if I had something to say. I knew I had to be careful; Milly was still a serving officer.

I opened my mouth and out it poured, the pain, the betrayal. I was like Zeus; I was throwing lightning bolts in quick succession. Lava was flowing through my veins. The boss just sat there, eyes wide. He absorbed every bit of anger I had; thanked me for my input and wrote in his little book. I would get my 'Dedication to the Service Certificate'.

October 27th was the date of the meeting, As of the 18th of January, as I write this page, I have received nothing. 83 days and not one person has walked to a computer, pressed a button and printed my certificate. Phileas Fogg went around the world in 80 days in 1872, but the police force can't send a certificate to someone who served for 19 years.

I gave my life to the force, but now I don't care what type of job I end up in; my family will never take second place again. They will always come first. I know they are always there for me in a way no employer will ever be. What's next for me? I don't know. I'm retired at 44 years old.

My brother and I used to laugh at dad and mock him as he turned 60. We used to shout 'Bus Pass' to him in foolish voices. It was all fun; it was a Pearson thing. We were preparing him for his retirement; reminding Papa Bear that he was getting older. Now he's gone and I'm the one who's retired, but without the bus pass.

I still hear his voice shouting at me as I teased him. I had no idea then about retirement or what it meant to someone. Now it's different. If I was rich, I suppose I would enjoy being retired, having fun, doing as I wanted; I'm not sure. I then think about the millionaires, famous actors and sports stars. They have all the money they want, but it doesn't mean they are happy. I think there is something about working and earning money that appeals to me.

I was brought up to think of work as important. 'Nothing is free in this life,' I was told, and working is the way to make sure you can pay your way. Get your ass out there and crack on; retirement isn't fun. Sitting and watching trivial TV all day long; missing the friends you spent 19 years with, feeling worthless. Trust me; it's not fun at all.

Since retirement I have walked, run and pottered around the house and garden. Then my book was released and exceeded all of my expectations. I may have mental issues, but it doesn't stop me from wanting to find success. I still want to win. I want to make a difference in peoples' lives. I want to achieve.

I know it will take me time to change from the robotisation of the force, and the person I was then, to become myself again. It will take me a while to achieve that. I have spent a long time being someone else and I'm looking forward to being Ben again. I will keep putting out Twitter messages to make people laugh, and I will do all I can to get organisations to stand up and be counted where mental health is concerned.

I'm also going to pay a lot of attention to Milly and my two children. Milly's life has changed massively now that I'm not in the police force. We have literally changed roles. A weight has been lifted from her when it comes to juggling the kids around shifts. I know the strain it put on her to go to work and come home as I left for work, and then spend the day watching the kids. This was both of our lives, day in, day out. Days out together with our children were very rare. It was mentally and physically exhausting.

Milly was forced to stay in front line policing on an opposite shift to me to make it work. Now, she can change that and arrange a less punishing shift pattern. Long night shifts were crippling, but now she can leave those behind her. There will still be shift work, but it won't be as intense.

I'm pleased that Milly can now think about her own career and not be held back because of irregular shift patterns. It was never an option for her before. Kids, and being a police mum don't go well together. She has had to miss school events, putting the kids to bed at night, and other important milestones in their lives.

Sometimes, Milly and I have had only three 'family days' together in ten weeks. We made it work, but it was hard. We see each other more than ever now, and I have taken on a more active role with the children. I get them up when Milly is on 'lates.' I do the school runs which I enjoy; I get to know the other parents in the playground. I see what my kids are doing at school, who they are playing with, and the teachers who look after them.

Milly will tell you things have changed since the book came out. People approach her and tell her what the book has meant to them; how it has impacted on their lives and opened their eyes to what police officers do daily. These include people who have known us for a long time. There were many things in the book that they didn't know.

People are more than willing to tell Milly when they are struggling. They know she will never judge them, and she relates to them. She understands what they are going through. The number of messages I get from people suffering through mental illness has amazed Milly. Yet somehow, it doesn't surprise her, she has seen it all with me. I know she is very proud of me; she sees me sitting for hours replying to the messages and telling them to speak out. The message is powerful.

I can't remember the last time I valued life as much as I do now. I'm home with the kids most of the time and you can't put a value on that. I love taking them out bike riding around the parks, while I walk slowly behind them.

Does it sound strange to you when I say I look around and admire the simple things? Strangely, I'm obsessed with the bluebells that grow in early spring. We go for walks, and I just start looking for them; I keep saying to myself this is what mad people do. Well, if it is, I'm proud to say I do it all the time.

I take in smells, colours, feeling textures on plants and trees while my children chat away, bickering behind me. These are the things you miss out on so much when you lead a stressful life continually on the move. You fail to look at the little detail in things and the beauty that surrounds us in the natural world. It was summed up to me a few years ago.

I was reminiscing on being a kid, convinced that summers were much warmer and longer than now. Why did a year seem to take 18 months, and why did it seem to take an eternity to get from the beginning of December to Christmas day? A wise person told me it was because as a child you have nothing more to think about, or to do than play out and watch time go slowly by. You don't have to worry about health, money or bills, and the rest of the tedium that takes up your adult life. As a child, you were bounding with energy and just wanted the best out of life. Then you hit 40, and you started counting down the days until you retired. You thought about your pension; Would it be enough? You became consumed with how you'd manage; what you'd do to pass your time.

With the stress of policing now removed from my life, I am opening my eyes again to the world around me. I feel like an inquisitive child, seeing and touching things for the first time. I Ask myself why it's taken me over 36 years to find its value again.

I want to live a simple life now; I want to forget the horrific, long traffic queues to get to work; setting off at a ridiculous hour, just in case I get stuck in one during my seven-mile journey. Now I just don't care, I'm happy to stuff my wallet and phone in my pocket and set of walking. I don't know where, I've not packed any lunch, no cheese sandwiches or cold lemonade to drink; I'll just go wherever life takes me.

I know my danger filter is not working correctly, but it feels good not to care. It feels like I'm 10 years old again on my way to call for my friend so we can play out on our BMX's. I look back now and see how foolish I was to see such things as only possible in childhood. It will never happen again.

If I can give anyone any advice, it would be, never take what you have for granted, I did, and it burnt me to my core. Live your life for you and your family. But most important; it's the simple things that matter the most.

Finale - IT'S OKAY, NOT TO BE OKAY

I don't shy away from having a mental illness, and I never try to pretend to Milly. She knows the days I am okay and the days I am not okay. It may seem that all this publicity is going on, and some people may think I'm wallowing in the glory, but believe me, I am not. People speaking out can only be a good thing, and more need to feel confident to do that.

I find it hard to believe that I'm not the breadwinner anymore. It's really tough. I always prided myself on being able to provide for my family. I'm now a stay-at-home dad. Milly now calls me her 'house bitch.' I know it's 2021, but I'm a Yorkshire man and still see my role as providing for my family. It's not the norm for me to see my partner working all the shifts she has to, whilst I can do nothing to relieve her of the burden.

I have no option, and she knows that. I'm deemed unfit for regular work. The current pandemic isn't helping me either. I'm someone who thrives on physical interaction, and that has stopped. Going to the gym has been halted due to Covid, and I loved doing my work outs. I took up running, but a lump I have found, has meant I can't at the moment; so that has stopped as well. Prior to this, I used to run between four and eight kilometres per day. It cleared my head; made me feel better.

Milly knows without that release I sit and fester at nights. The kids are in bed, and I'm sat alone with my thoughts. Sometimes I feel a need to phone her and tell her I am feeling low. On a positive side, I don't have the stress of thinking I have to go back into policing; I don't have the same panic attacks. I don't hyperventilate at the thought of going back into the police station; I don't have the worry of wondering if they will pension me off, although I've been told

I am pensioned off, but the process isn't complete. I trust that it will be soon.

It upsets Milly that I struggle with my identity, especially when I refer to myself as a traffic cop or watch something on TV I can't deal with. It has to be turned off. Adapting to civilian life has been and is hard. Some friends I thought I had, have turned out not to be friends. I have made new friends, though, but I now understand what it means when people refer to 'real friends.

What will the future hold for us? At the moment we are stuck in limbo. I await my pension; I don't know if I will ever be able to return to full-time employment. Both issues are unsettling. We are playing a waiting game. I still need to have the detailed therapy that helps to heal me.

I know I will never be the same Ben who Milly met; I wonder if I will ever go back to the old Ben. It impacts on me. Milly thinks I am more compassionate now, perhaps she is right. I now know the cost of suffering a hidden illness.

I have so many unanswered questions. I need answers, but I know it will take time before I get them. I need closure to move on. I want to focus on my recovery and move forward. It will be a new life for us both, but as a family I know we will deal with whatever comes next.

I'll never fully leave the force behind; there are too many memories, good and bad. There will always be triggers. Milly still works as a police officer and I loved my job, despite what happened, and so does Milly. I just want institutional changes to be made. I want them to learn from their mistakes with me and ensure they are not repeated for others.

I try hard not to be bitter, but sometimes I feel that way. I apologise to all those reading this if this comes over too strongly; It isn't meant to. Recently, I have been contacted by a man called Josh, and persuaded by him to get my message out to a wider audience. He introduced me to 'You Tube,' and has helped me to start my channel. Initially, I thought this was too much for me. I now see it's reaching a different type of audience, but the message is always the same.

Whatever point you are at in your life, you can change. It's never too late. Don't forget your journey, but know whatever pain you have been through, you cannot let it stop you going where you want to go. Someone once said to me, 'How do you live a perfect life?' Well, you can't, but you can live your life, be happy in yourself, and be kind to others. It's not too much to ask, really.

Every day has become an unwritten day, as I step outside with my children, I know I can decide what I want them to do and see, and whatever that is, I want it to be fun. I have so many demons holding my shoulders every day, restraining me, but I can see the joy in my children's eyes, as they grow and look towards the future.

During the winter I went sledging with them. I watched as they slid down the snow ramp they had made with the neighbours, and I could see how much fun it was for them. My children were screaming with laughter. Happiness filled the air, and I realised in that moment, I was happy, but the weight I carry every day was still a heavy burden. I try to visualise where I've gone wrong and what I could do now to change it. What do I change? I don't know who I am. What am I now? It's a question I ask myself.

What do I tell people who ask me what I do? Am I a house husband? If so, what am I when the kids are at school? Recently I had to get my car insured and was asked what my profession was. I had to stop and think. It's strange; the last 19 years I've always put 'Police' and 'Law and Order.' It was automatic, built into me. It's just the same as when you meet new people, friends of a friend. 'Hi, I'm Ben.' 'Hi Ben, what do you do for a living then?' 'Err I'm a Pol........ erm no I'm not. Am I an author?' I've worked hard and have a book published, which is a number one bestseller. Does that make me an author then? It sounds so surreal saying that. Imagine meeting people from my school in a reunion.

'Hi, remember me, I'm Ben.... the author.' I can hear them coughing into their hands, thinking, 'bullshit.' So, who am I? I've co-authored two books now. Some authors never get past the first, so YES, I am an author.

People ask me if I would go back into the police, and do I regret anything? Do I regret authoring a book? Should I be working at a local supermarket, or delivering car parts? No, I don't regret it; I don't regret a thing. I'm proud of my books. If something happens to me, I have a legacy to leave for others to read. I think that's what it's all about. Kids go to school to learn, we learnt in the police every day. We grow old, still learning. So, if someone picks up my book, reads it, and feels or understands what I've felt, then I'm happy. I know they will learn from that.

I'm a long way from perfect, I don't know the answers any more than you do, far from it. But I refuse to settle for second best, I want to be the best me I can be, poorly or not. If people still want to read or hear my stories, I'll keep telling them. I've learned that the best outlook on life is to refuse to settle for less than you deserve. You make the choices of who you want to be, no one else, and if you're not where you want to be right now, sort it. You control your life and your destiny, no one else. If you want to reach for the stars, or go for your dreams, then do it. I know I will.

All of these thoughts play out in my head as I'm getting snowballs thrown at me, I'm trying to smile but then I think about Isaak, I keep wondering where he is now? What's he, and I smile, I have to, but it's so hard to have fun when your mind is elsewhere. I'm so determined to put some of these thoughts to bed. If only I can find the answers; get some closure, no matter how small. I have found it hard to learn self-forgiveness.

Isaak is the guiltless lad from the Subaru crash that occurred years ago. He constantly played on my mind, and I kept telling myself I should have aborted the pursuit earlier or gone back to the station as I almost did. In 'Handcuffed Emotions,' I told of Isaak, a total innocent who lost his legs. I told of the nightmares I had of him, and how I blamed myself, and would never forgive myself. It's the not knowing what's happened to him that's the worst. Your mind tells you all sorts. Is he in some drug den, struggling to come to terms with his accident? Has he made a success of his life? Not having the answers, I need is soul destroying.

It's a big issue for anyone in the emergency services, whether it be the firefighters who cut the bodies from the wreckage, the paramedics who deal with the injured before passing them on to the doctors and surgeons, or police officers, who will charge or report, deal with incidents, and send files to the CPS. The problem being, none of us sees the job to its conclusion, so I never really know the outcome. We never speak with the victims 2–5 years down the line to see how life is treating them. Are they now a failure because of actions we took; have they given up on life? Or have they made a better version of themselves and come out on top?

We don't forget these people; we wonder where, why and what, but never get to know. I felt like that about Isaak. Then, one day, I opened my Twitter account to see I had a message from Isaak's mother. I want to share with you what I read because it changed my life in a single moment. She told me how positive Isaak was. He now has a B.Sc. with Honours in music, and a five-year-old son. She ended by saying, 'he may have lost a limb, but it does not stop him.'

When that arrived, I broke down in tears; to know he was happy and thriving. Isaak lost a limb, I lost peace of mind, but like him I will not stop until I am well again, and mental health is out in the open for all to see.

I want to end this chapter by telling you my feelings as I write:

I can't reach out of the book and personally shake everyone's hand who has purchased it. I can't give you all a cuddle, but I want you to know that every one of you has had a massive, positive impact on my life. You have made me smile on the darkest nights. You have made me believe, when I couldn't see a future. You are the reason I will continue with my dreams and goals, and I cannot thank you enough. All I can say is, THANK YOU, THANK YOU ALL SO MUCH.

MEET THE AUTHORS

Ben Pearson has spent the last 19 years of his life fighting crime. He was part of the elite 'Roads Policing Unit' of West Yorkshire Police, featured in the hit TV series 'Police Interceptors,' showing on Channel 5.

As a decorated officer, he has driven in the fastest, most dangerous pursuits, arrested murderers, rapists and high-profile burglars. He has taken down the most violent offenders and brought them to justice. As told in the number 1 best seller, 'Handcuffed Emotions - A police interceptor's drive into darkness.'

'Hotel Tango 23 - Responding to the Unknown' is the sequel, expanding on Ben's policing career. It tells the heart stopping stories of the adrenaline fuelled life of a highly trained police officer. The book is fast-paced and gives an insight into the world of law enforcement; the good, the bad, and the evil. Respond to the unknown alongside Ben as you experience high speed 'blue light' runs, violent arrests, and hard to believe stories of criminal activity, to his days without a badge and rehabilitation from a premature career ending.

Patricia Sutcliffe is a published author and has been a life-writer/ biographer for many years. Her first writing success came when she was just ten years old, winning a national school story writing competition. Since that time Pat has continued to write, publishing both fictional and non-fictional works. She is an active member of 'Harrogate Writers' Circle' and has received 'highly commended' accolades about her work. Pat has also won several writing competitions, and is a member of the Society of Authors.

Her book reviews from readers are excellent, as are her commendations from clients and can be read on her website: www.patriciasutcliffeauthor.com Her qualifications include an Oxford University course in 'Advanced Life Writing', MA in Strategic Decision Making and a B.Ed. in English.

ANDY'S MAN CLUB

In mid-2016, nine men met in a small room in the archetypal Yorkshire town of Halifax with a simple aim of talking through their issues and helping each other deal with their mental health. All of those in attendance agreed there was a magic in the room that needed to be shared. This was the start of a movement that has grown faster than anyone first involved could ever have imagined. Fast forward five years and 'ANDY'S MAN CLUB' now has groups at over 40 locations, across three constituent countries of the United Kingdom.

'ANDY'S MAN CLUB' takes its name from Andrew Roberts, a man who sadly took his own life, aged 23, in early 2016. Andy's family had no inkling he was suffering or struggling to the extent he would do this. As a result, they looked deeper into male suicide and men's mental health. They soon discovered that male suicide is the biggest killer of men under 50, with Male mental health surrounded by well-ingrained cultural stigma in the UK.

Elaine Roberts and Luke Ambler are Andy's mum and brother-in-Law. Together, they came up with the idea of

'ANDY'S MAN CLUB', a group of where men, aged 18 and above, can speak openly about their mental health in a judgement-free, non-clinical environment. Groups now operate nationwide and are completely volunteer led, with the vast majority of group facilitators having first interacted with 'ANDY'S MAN CLUB' when they came through the door as a service user. Over a thousand men now use their service on a weekly basis.

With an army of over 200 volunteers on board, the movement is continuing to grow on a weekly basis.

Luke Ambler, co-founder of Andy's Man Club, said:

'Ben has been a friend of 'Andy's Man Club' for a long time now, and his story is an inspiration to all of us at the group. The more people who raise awareness of Mental Health and how important talking is, the closer we get to reducing male suicide and helping more men.' To attend 'ANDY'S MAN CLUB', drop us an e-mail: info@andysmanclub.co.uk

Printed in Great Britain
by Amazon